Ever your own,
Johnnie
Britain, 1938-42

By the same author:

Ever your own, Johnnie
North Africa, 1942-43

Ever your own, Johnnie,
Sicily and Italy, 1943-45

Ever your own, Johnnie
Britain, 1938-42

Letters by John Kemp,

whilst serving in
53rd, 88th, and 76th H.A.A. Regiments, Royal Artillery.

Edited, preface, and commentary by
Nick Kemp

Published by Nick Kemp
2016

In memory of
John and Peggy

First printed 2016

ISBN 978-1-326-59785-6

nickkempbooks@yahoo.co.uk

Gnr John Kemp, a pencil cartoon self-portrait, 1938.

In the background is an anti-aircraft gun, whilst to the left the figures depicted are possibly men around a Predictor and a height finder.

Contents

Editor's preface

John Kemp voluntarily enlisted in the Territorial Army on 30 March 1938 at the age of twenty because he, like many others, feared war between Nazi Germany and Britain was inevitable. He was at this time much in love with Peggy whom he had met in 1936 and who was to become his wife in May 1940. Of the letters written by John to Peggy between July 1938 and December 1945 four hundred and eighty eight survive, telling of John's day-to-day life in the T.A. and subsequently on active service in the Army in Britain, North Africa, Sicily, and Italy. Intermittently from October 1943 John also kept a diary together with retrospective accounts of his life whilst overseas. This book, however, covers only the period from 1938 to November 1942, the darkening days leading up to war, the Phoney War, the Dunkirk crisis, the Battle of Britain, and his Regiment's preparations for the Allied Forces' invasion of North Africa. His accounts of life in North Africa, and then Sicily and Italy will be published in subsequent books.

I came into possession of John's letters and diaries following his death, and quickly realised on reading just one or two of these that there was a vivid story to be told in his own words about defending one's country and of the pain of being forced apart from loved ones. I also quickly realised how little I knew about his war record: whilst he had recounted a few stories during his life of his wartime service, the occasion when he was machine gunned whilst in Italy, about a lucky near miss from a bursting German shell, he in fact gave away little information that would allow those who had not been with him to realise the reality, sometimes grim, of what he had experienced. Whilst John had at some point in his retirement revisited his letters and added a few margin notes on those originating from the early years of the war, these notes were tantalisingly missing in detail. Looking further into his letters and diaries, my curiosity was raised to know more about where he had been, and the engagements in which he had taken part, especially so as much of his writing deliberately omitted such detail to prevent 'idle talk' that could potentially compromise wartime security. On visiting the National Archives at Kew and trawling the available official War Diaries it became evident that there was a context in which to place John's letters and diaries to give them relevance and substance, and to explain some of the more, deliberately, obscure entries. Whilst the documents have generally been transcribed as written by John some of the original texts contain overlapping accounts, these, for the purposes of this book, being edited and merged to provide continuity and to avoid repetition. More personal passages, plainly meant only for Peggy's eyes, have been omitted!

I very much hope that what is recounted here through the transcription of John's words and in the commentary and explanatory notes I have placed alongside them, goes in some way to providing an understanding and recognition of the sacrifice of the time and lives of those that served in the forces and of their families at home, and that this was not in vain for the very great freedom that we all have today.

Nick Kemp
March 2016

An introduction, in John's own words

"For several years before 1939 it had been clearly demonstrated that Adolf Hitler was intent on territorial gains in Europe, and possibly the world. His considerable achievement as an orator, particularly on Germany's bad treatment at the Treaty of Versailles, had accumulated for him his nation's acclaim as their undisputed leader. Daily papers were full of Hitler's speeches, and I can recall the feeling of apprehension and dread at these reports. Wireless news broadcasts were avidly absorbed. The prospect of war hung like a cloud over any thoughts of future prospect and planning.

I attended London Polytechnic from 1936 with the intention of taking the qualifying exams that would subsequently lead to my practising as an architect. I recall the continuous topic of conversation, "Do you think there's going to be a war?" and the subsequent discussion that would follow. There were a number of depletions as students left to join the Forces. Posters to encourage enlisting in the T.A. were a common sight, advertisements appearing all over London and elsewhere saying, "Join the Territorial Army".

During the period from 1936 to 1939 Peggy and I attended many dances. We met many young people of our own age – many of the male members were, or soon became, members of the T.A. Little persuasion was required for my friend Bob and I to join up with them. On a date that has been forgotten, Bob and I became Gunners Hall and Kemp as members of 158th (City of London) A.A. Battery, 53rd Brigade, Royal Artillery. Peggy was extremely concerned, and remonstrated with me because I had joined without first consulting her. When matters settled down she told me it was because she did not want to lose me.

T.A. parades were on Tuesday evenings, with periodic obligatory weekend "camps" at H.Q. Evening parades, I recall, were from 19.00hrs to 21.00hrs, consisting of a variety of activities, including rifle drill, dismounted cavalry drill, lectures on guns and ammunition, and, treat of all treats, gun drill on a sadly worn static World War I 3" A.A. gun. This had its amusing side, since it was supposed to be mobile, and there were hilarious sessions of taking the gun "out of action" on its wheels.

Prior to the meeting of Chamberlain and Hitler in Munich, reservists and T.A. were called up. Our battery mounted guns at Richmond Park at Sheen gate, where we were stationed in tents for three weeks. Apart from the obvious initial distress and anxiety, this was an enthralling experience. Returning to civvie street was an anti-climax. We had enjoyed a short-lived life of being soldiers, and visits to the Bull at Sheen.

Peggy and I, having known each other for only three years, were to be parted following the declaration of war in August 1939 until New Year's Eve in 1945, with a total of six weeks leave together during this period. The purpose of these words is not to provide a historical education, but to record how we managed somehow to keep our reason by writing regularly to each other."

Extract from a document written by John Kemp in the 1980s.

Prelude, 1938

Sandhurst Way, Sanderstead, Sunday 3 July 1938

My darling Sweetheart,

Well darling, how is everything? I do hope you are comfortable in your hotel and that the weather is exceptionally good. I am longing for your letter tomorrow to know how you are enjoying it.

Bob and I got back from parade tonight at about 7 o'clock both feeling terribly dirty and tired. The uniform seemed to add considerably to our discomfort. We felt so sticky that we both had a bath when we got back tonight. And you can now say that we both feel and are much cleaner.

I suppose I had really better start with my actions since yesterday morning and then shall miss nothing. I went up to town as usual and did a really hard morning's work on some important stuff for Pearce Duff's factory[1]. It was an uneventful journey home.

I was just settling down to a little gardening when Monty Percy rolled up in a most derelict car. I should honestly think it was the first car Mr Austin ever made. He stayed and had some tea and went shortly

---

[1] Blancmange powder makers, Spa Road, Bermondsey. John at this time was training to be an architect, and held the position of Junior Assistant at Lawrence Kennard, Architects.

1

afterwards. Pop and I spent most of the evening tidying odds and ends in the garage and garden, and when Bob and Ruth returned home from the speed trials in Brighton, Bob and I started on our uniforms in a wild endeavour to get them looking ship shape. We started these about 10 o'clock and after working solidly without a break went up to bed at a little before 2 o'clock and boy were we glad to get into bed. The polishing of those belts is no simple matter, believe you me.

We were both up about 7.30 this morning getting the perishing uniform on. The boots seemed to fit.

It's been a hard day. We've been loading the gun solidly all day long. The weather has been sultry, and the uniform is anything but cooling. What it's going to be like at camp heaven above knows.

Now the most important question of all. When are you coming home?

Remember me to all, ever yours and lovingly,

John

R.A. Practice Camp, Weybourne, Holt, Norfolk, 19 July 1938

Darling Sweetheart

We've got a few spare minutes, so I'll write you now, but cannot promise when it will be finished. Well. Peg, I've some bad news for you. Coming up in the car, we got a puncture just outside Newmarket. This we mended very successfully by changing wheels and putting on the spare. We went on about 30 miles more, and noticed a knocking in the engine. Without a word of warning the whole engine seized up solid. We had to send to a local garage and have the car towed into Newmarket, having already pushed it about a mile.

We managed to get to camp O.K., and arrived on the dot. Apart from the breakdown, the journey was not enjoyable. We had lunch at Royston I think it was. We rang up the garage last night, and found the cost of repairing the car will not be worth the value of it. So we have asked the bloke in the garage to see if he can sell it for us. He seems to think he will be able to do so. So it's not so bad.

Bob Maurice (one of the blokes in the car) and I were collared on arrival for fatigue work. We had to dig a trench round one of the H.Q. tents for disposal of rainwater. Believe me it did rain the first night! And most of yesterday morning. After digging we were detailed off to draw blankets and straw for the palliasses (mattresses). We spent Sunday evening in the canteen. We've got a spanking place here. We have an excellent site right on the coast with about a quarter of a mile to the gun park where we shoot. We turned in fairly early on Sunday but did not go to sleep until late after much singing and yarning – (it's terrible hard to write. There's no privacy at all here, and the blokes here are very amusing). As I say, yesterday morning it rained. In the afternoon we went down to the gun park and I had my first experience of gunfire. It was damn good fun, it really was. Really, in spite of the fact that we should have felt tired yesterday, we were as fresh as new paint. To prove it we walked into Sherringham last night (about five miles) – not having the car is certainly going to cut down expenses a hell of a lot. And I feel sure that, had we had the car last night, we could not have enjoyed it more. Not having the car has limited our scope outside the camp, as we have only Sherringham within walking distance.

We had roll call at 5.45 this morning. It was really grand at that time and has been all day – I'm as brown as a berry. We marched up and down on the parade ground all morning, and went to the gun park for firing all the afternoon (more thrills). We have just finished tea and I'm writing this in the canteen.

I miss you terribly sweetheart. Still, I hope that the fortnight will soon pass. Hope you will excuse more darling, will try to write better and more soon.

Tons and tons of love sweetheart,

yours ever,

Wiggie.

Gunner John Kemp, probably Weybourne Camp anti-aircraft gunnery range, July 1938.

23 September 1938
T.A. troops called up following the declaration of a State of
Emergency by the British Government in response to Germany's
annexation of Austria, and its demands for Sudetenland
autonomy in Czechoslovakia.

No 2 Section/158 Bty 53,
C. of L. Brigade, Sheen Gate, Richmond Park SW14.

Tuesday *(undated, but believed to be 27 September 1938)*[2]

My Own Darling Gorgeous and Eternal Sweetheart,

At long last I have the opportunity of dropping you a line. At the moment (9.30) we are in our tent and I am writing this by the light of a feeble candle. I'll start from the beginning and go right through. Old Bob and I had a wonderful run up to the White City, made in just over ½ hr. We crashed five red lights. When we got there we had several forms to fill in. The rush and turmoil was so great that there was no medical examination etc. We loaded guns until about 11.15 and then came down here, getting here about 12 o'clock last night. Then it started to pour in torrents (as it is now) – the next job was to unload the guns, still in the rain. We had coffee (jolly good) and sandwiches and turned in about 3 o'clock. Last night we were billeted in a sort of stable affair and slept 12 men in a room 10ft x 10ft. Most uncomfortable!!! We had reveille at 10 o'clock this morning followed by breakfast. The food is damn good. All day we have been putting up tents in which we now are – digging trenches and latrines etc. It's been a very hectic day. All the other blokes in this tent are now asleep except Bob – he's writing too. It's a lovely site here. Right in the park, actually in the trees. I was green with envy this morning to see people riding. Wonder when we'll ride together again my sweetheart?

---

[2] John was called out for military service, as Gunner Kemp, on 26 September. Troops were stood down 8 October.

Wonder what you are doing now? Maybe in the theatre. I can't say how rotten I felt last night about it all and was completely unable to express it. Do tell Liz how sorry I am. Darling, if you get a chance I'd love to see you. We will be getting leave once we are all straight here, and I'll see you then somewhere and somehow. I love you so angel. By the way, if you go up to my place will you do me a favour? I left my elephant[3] in the left hand inside pocket of my grey suit, and am lost without it. I wonder how you got on last night? I'm afraid Mother was feeling the whole affair very badly. Poor old darling, she was upset, and you seemed so brave darling. Bless you. I shall never forget your kiss.

I'd love to know what's going on in the outside world. We're isolated here. Haven't even got any beer. The candle is getting very low and I can hardly see, so will have to close – with all my very fondest love sweetheart – I love you so.

Ever your loving sweetheart,

John

---

30 September 1938
Munich Agreement signed (dated 29 September).

---

[3] Believed to be an ivory charm given to John by Peggy as a keepsake.

Defence of Britain

1939

---

21 August 1939
T.A. anti-aircraft units mobilised.

24 August 1939
John Kemp called up.[4]

Saturday 26 August 1939 *(postcard)*

We are at Hurlingham Polo Ground, SW6 (just off Putney Bridge)[5].
Bob written Ruth. Ring her up. All my love darling, write later,

John.

---

[4] John and other troops from 158 Battery had been transferred to 282 Battery,
88th H.A.A Regiment, on 21 April 1939. They were subsequently embodied
into the regiment on 24 August, on the day of him being called up.
[5] Map references for this and other gun sites on which John served are
included in Appendix 1.

1 September 1939
Germany invades Poland.

3 September 1939
Britain declares war on Germany.

Gunners Bob Hall and John Kemp (right) at Hurlingham Polo Ground,
September 1939

No2 Hurlingham Polo Ground, 28 September 1939[6]

Peggy darling,

After last night's abruptly ended letter, I'll try to cover the ground I was unable to. As I have already told you, we are on guard at the moment, and so there are times in between the changing of the guard when we get a slack period, which is at present. The duties consist of mounting a fresh guard every 2 hrs: I have been put in as N.C.O. in charge of relieving the old sentries, which means that I have to change them every 2 hrs. During the night, of course, this was not so funny as it meant turning out as soon as I got some sleep. This however was not so serious as it may sound, as the N.C.O. in charge of the guard took over from 2 o'clock to 4 o'clock. So I was able to get some sleep.

Today it has been very pleasant out in the sun. Thank heaven it has not been wet. We did have some slight rain the first day here, but I was fortunate enough to be able to keep under cover. The old hands today are really beginning to settle down, and this, more or less rest, has been rather welcome in that respect, as the hands become so tender right down to the finger tips that you can only just take a match from a box. Talk about dirt, I swear I shall never be able to get my hands clean. They are absolutely invisible under a film of gun oil and grease.

We spent yesterday afternoon before mounting guard cleaning up the guns. Damn good fun really. We have four 3.7s here, and they are beginning to look most efficient as the sand bags gradually rise round them. Tonight at 6 o'clock we are supposed to knock off and have a rest period for the next 24 hrs, but until all these sandbags are filled, I can't see any rest period yet. But still, that is very enjoyable, and we have some damn good fun filling these bags and rushing them from the other side of the road. We have our own Military Policemen here, and they hold up the traffic while a crowd of half clad scruffy dirty looking lads, numbering anything up to fifty in number push a huge trailer from the back of a lorry across the road at full canter. The noise they make is unbelievable. We have crowds at the gate just to watch

---

[6] John was promoted to Lance Bombardier on 4 September.

them come over. The speed they do it at is so amazing that it amazes me no one has been injured.

The food here is absolutely wonderful, and we have had a full complement of blankets etc. from the first night we arrived, and then some spare. So different from last September. I begin to think that the old country is <u>really</u> ready. From where I'm sitting in the guard tent I can see blokes piling up sand bags as hard as they can go. About 99% are completely stripped to the waist and have a pair of slacks and gym shoes on (as per illustration).

I can see backs so sunburnt that I cannot possibly imagine how they will be able to put a shirt on, let alone lie down on their backs. Here comes that trailer again. What a row. Rattling through a cloud of dust it comes tearing across the road and about one hundred yards across the field to the guns. If I were not in the same position myself I should imagine they honestly stink!

ANY THREVINGHAM GUNNER

Well my angel, I wonder how you are? It will be wonderful to see you again and I feel so sure that the time is not as far off as any of us imagine.

Well my sweetheart, for the present, I must stop. If you get time, please write me, I do so love to hear how you are.

Tons and tons of love my darling,

ever your very own sweetheart,

Johnnie

Hurlingham, September 1939. A ten man gun detachment of 282/88 H.A.A. Regt during a yellow alert. John Kemp seated centre without helmet.

Chingford[7], 7 November 1939

My own darling sweetheart,

Have just received your letter, for which I am more than grateful. It came as a wonderful surprise and refresher.

We returned from our week of mud on Sunday, and are now back at our old place. Peggy darling, I've never in all my life felt so horribly depressed. What I'd give to see you again is absolutely beyond measure. We arrived back here in the afternoon on Sunday, and the place seems

---

[7] John's section of 282 Battery moved to Chingford 30 September, where construction of gun site ZE17 (Beaulieu) was commenced, this including Lewis gun positions. A note added later to this letter by John indicates the address for the letter as being "Freezy Water, Royal Forest Hotel", this being a billet in Chingford, the regiment having previously been billeted in the Masonic Hall, Chingford. The battery was designated to defend 'vulnerable points' (V.P.s), being munitions factories at Waltham Abbey and Enfield. John was by the time of this letter an Acting Bombardier, having been promoted on 9 October.

horribly empty. At the moment there are two other sections out on the stint we were on last week. On top of which there are about 75% of our section away on seven days or 48 hrs leave, and of course I'm about the sole remaining member of the gang left. It all seems so pointless to keep about thirty blokes here, the remainder of the two sections, just to make fatigues for each other. They only seem to be finding work for people, work that could be avoided if they gave us all leave. We have only these fatigues to do here, and there is nothing in the army more boring or depressing than a fatigue. Actually fatigues are given as punishment in the ordinary way. On top of it all I can see no signs of the leave I had anticipated under three or four weeks under the present system. After this week I understand that there will be no more eight hours or forty-eight hours. On Friday of this week I am supposed to be going away for a course of gunnery – where I don't know. But at least it will be much better than this awful inactivity. Pegs, if it goes on much more it will drive me mad.

After the course is over I understand we are once again going out for a week on some caper we were on last week. If only we were stationed nearer home I could perhaps see you in the evenings. Even if you were not on this A.R.P.[8] work, you might be able to come and stay for a few days somewhere near. God! It's awful not being able to see you angel.

We returned to the hotel here to find that the telephone is out of order, so I have been unable to phone you, and since when we have been unable to get out. There is a rumour that we may be able to have some leave tonight, so consequently I hope I shall be able to phone you then. Please let me have a list of times when you are not on duty so that I can fix things up if I get a chance. You never know in the army.

All the love and kisses in the world sweetheart, and remember I love you forever,

Ever your own,

John.

---

[8] Air Raid Precautions. Peggy at this time was an A.R.P. ambulance driver.

The Haunted House[9], 24 November 1939

My own darling,

At least I have a few spare minutes to write to you. We returned from our course on Wednesday, and you may be pleased to know that Johnnie is now in charge of a gun station[10] – absolutely, without anyone else. There are fifteen men, and at the moment, everything is running beautifully, and I feel really my old self again, plenty to do, although not much time to do it in. That rain yesterday spoilt things rather, but it is much more comfortable where I am at the moment, we at least have a hut which makes everything much more cheerful.

That journey back on Monday was very long, and to pass the time I took off my uniform and cleaned it on the train. Of course I had to run for the train!

Have just received your letter darling, which is as usual very sweet and my sincerest thanks, angel. You mention something about an air raid warning?? Had I heard about it?? Darling, you should know me better than to give away secrets!! Tell you about it when I next see you.

The course finished up with an exam. Not too clever. Thought I'd done very well until I heard what the others had written. Still, I don't think it was too bad. With your letter, I also had a letter from Ruth. She has absolutely fallen in love with your jersey (or whatever you call it). Says she has never seen you in anything she likes better.

Incidentally, they have started the seven days leave again, so hope mine will be coming along soon, but cannot give you more details yet. Hope

---

[9] Location unknown, but possibly still the billet at Royal Forest Hotel. The Regimental H.Q. had moved to Crews Hill Golf Club, Enfield, on 20 November. At this time 282 Battery took over the Burnt Farm, Cuffley (ZW3) gun site, less one troop, that being based at Waltham Abbey (ZE11) in an L.A.A. role, prior to H.A.A. guns being delivered, after which it rejoined the battery.

[10] From notes made by John Kemp, this was a Lewis gun, training having been given on the course to which John refers, it being held at Royal Small Arms factory in Enfield. Lewis gun positions were a feature of H.A.A. gun sites at this time due to a shortage of heavy guns.

you will excuse writing, but the light is very bad, and I'm on my knees as we have no table.

Well my darling, all the love from your own gunner boy, and writing again soon,

Ever your own,

Johnnie.

Bdr John Kemp with twin Bren guns on a Motley mounting, used for light anti-aircraft defence, location unknown.

1940

Aberporth[11], 19 March 1940[12]

Peggy darling, once again the opportunity arises, so am taking it to make sure of writing to you today, in case it does not arise again today. Very little news since I wrote to you last. Except that it looks very much to me as though we shall be here until after Easter. The weather has been so bad that we have been unable to shoot since Friday. This rain is infuriating. At the moment it's pouring and does not look like clearing. Yesterday afternoon it was so impossible that we were dismissed at midday. On Saturday we moved into a new mess, which is most comfortable. We have two huts, one for eating, and one for a rest room. It's just these extra luxuries that make it worthwhile being a Sgt. We spent yesterday afternoon in the rest room, reading and sleeping. I still cannot shake off this sleepiness and nor can anyone else. We have a sherry party in our mess tonight to which we have invited all the officers. Should be quite good fun. I do feel annoyed about this b- weather, I had hoped to be home for Easter.

Bob has been sent on a further course with another fellow from the Bty. I must hand it to Robert, he has certainly worked hard for it and

---

[11] Gunnery training range, near Cardigan, the battery's training at this location being from 8 to 28 March. After returning, 282/88 H.A.A. Regt took over five Lewis gun sites at Cricklewood, before being redeployed at Bentley Priory.
[12] John was promoted to Lance Sergeant on 6 March 1940.

perhaps now he will get rewarded for the work. Well my angel, must close now. The wind at the moment is deafening, and blowing so hard it nearly blows you over!

Ever your own sweetheart,

Johnnie.

A ten man gun detachment of 282/88 H.A.A. Regt R.A. at Aberporth gunnery range. L/Sgt John Kemp second from left.

John Kemp (right) on his wedding day, with Bob Hall as best man,
1 May 1940

Wedding of John and Peggy, by special licence, 1 May 1940.
John and Peggy had decided to marry at short notice when it was believed that
John could be imminently posted abroad.

---

10 May 1940
Germany invades Holland, Belgium, and France.
Churchill becomes Prime Minister of Great Britain.

---

13 May 1940[13]

My own darling sweetheart,

After I had been round with the orderly Officer last night and returned to my billet it was getting on for eleven o'clock. Everyone else seemed to be in bed when I returned and so I could not have the light on long enough to write to you. So do hope you get this letter today.

Everything is very vague, but I can tell you just a little more news. The advance guard leaves tomorrow for Aldershot[14], and the rest of us follow on on Thursday – or at least that is how it stands at the moment, and I suppose that is all liable to alteration – when and where we go from there we have no idea. I have, however, an idea that we shall be going north somewhere, as we are being issued with two winter weight vests. I can't quite understand it. It may be Iceland or north of Scotland. One can never tell. One thing I feel sure of it's not Norway.

---

[13] No address is included on this letter. B.H.Q. on this date was located at Flower Lane, Mill Hill. Gun sites occupied were ZE13 Finsbury Park, and ZE18 Chingford. A margin note added at a later date on another letter would suggest John was possibly located at the latter.

[14] The Regiment was in preparation at this time to move to Southampton for service in France, instruction being issued on 16 May to assemble at Alma Barracks, Blackdown, prior to a proposed embarkation on 26 May. Although the Regiment reached Southampton, the move was abandoned due to the crisis developing in Dunkirk. The Battery departed Southampton on 28 May. The Regiment was again ordered to Southampton to embark, this time for Brest, on 11 June, but this was in turn cancelled on 18 June. John's section was then immediately redeployed at site ZS24 at Annerley Park, between Crystal Palace and Norwood, Surrey, prior to being ordered to the Gloucester/Brockworth Gun Defended Area (GDA) on 28 June.

19

It is so rotten being cooped up in a place like this with no leave. It all seems so useless really as we could have been on leave every day that we have had it stopped.

Beyond what I have told you Pegs I have absolutely no news. Perhaps no news is good news. We never know. Will write when more news dear.

All my love and kisses, ever your loving husband,

Johnnie

---

27 May – 4 June 1940
Evacuation of Allied troops from Dunkirk.

10 June 1940
Italy declares war on France and Britain.

22 June 1940
France signs Armistice with Germany.

Haydons Elm, Near Cheltenham, Glocs.[15]

Sunday 7 July 1940

My own darling Sweetheart,

Once again the wonderful chance of writing. We are now beginning to settle down here, and things are becoming more peaceful. This is such a wonderful part of the world. Lately for about the last three days the weather has not been so good, and we have had rain on several occasions, which held up our operations.

We've been very occupied lately making camouflage and hiding things away under trees and hedges. The camp is practically invisible now. I must say a very good job has been made of it.

---

[15] Gun site A12, Haydons Elm. On 7 July 88 H.A.A. Regt came under control of 5 A.A. Division.

I went into Gloucester again on Friday with Pudde Poole and another, Paddy Ryan. I cannot say I enjoyed it at all as it was spoilt by their meeting two women. Next time I get leave I shall not be going there with them. Honestly I was bored to tears. It always spoils things when this sort of thing happens and I would much prefer to go out with the lads.

I am still more thrilled with the scenery here more than I can say, and although it is such a ghastly hour I think the best time to see it is at dawn, which is in my opinion even better than sunset. Watched the sun coming up yesterday morning. It rises way back over some very flat country and a very stately belt of trees. But the colours yesterday were the best I've ever seen. Starting off with a pale salmon tint on the clouds looking as if they had small patches of powder puff sticking to them – the clouds themselves were a glorious dove grey which looked so beautiful against the streaks of bumpy salmon cloud and background of a bluey green. It made me feel so sad, as I watched it all changing into a pale lemon colour and ending up with a great splash of shining gold as the sun made its appearance above the trees. I felt I was watching the grand finale of some tragic play, as one or two remaining puffs of black night clouds scudded swiftly out of sight. By then the birds had reached a magnificent pitch of song. Silhouetted against all this grandeur and beauty was the cold grey streamlined mass of the Camel[16]. It did seem such a wicked contrast to nature's idea of beauty and living, and man's. And I kept wondering what man thinks he will ever gain by such hideous weapons over nature's glory.

We are still waiting for the first bang, and have had three or four of the enemy over our position during the time since I wrote to you last. I should imagine they were definitely reconnaissance planes, as they were flying at such a height, so maybe we can expect some action soon. I am rather beginning to hope that we do not go into action here. It would be absolute sacrilege to shatter the peacefulness of the countryside, but still I suppose it must be.

On several occasions we have heard heavy A.A. gunfire lately, and since I started this letter we heard one rather fierce burst of fire coming

---

[16] Army colloquialism for the 3" A.A. guns deployed on this site.

from the Bristol direction. The Camels and "eggs"[17] are quietly nestling under some very crafty camouflage at the moment, just like a dog straining on its leash waiting to bark its head off.

We had a call out this morning just after breakfast, and it caught me in a very awkward position. As a matter of fact, to put it quite crudely, I was being a good boy! I had to leave the throne room very hastily and dash across the field, wildly clutching pants and trousers, with shirt tails flapping in the breeze. It was a very inconsiderate time to come near us, as half the personnel were washing and shaving. There were many towels and half shaved faces on the guns this morning, someone even appeared in a pyjama coat, where it came from I don't know, but it looked very funny to see a pyjama clad being in a tin hat streaking across the field flat out. But it was all of no use as the Jerry passed overhead above the clouds, and we were unable to get at him. So we returned to our various toilets, and parade was put forward half an hour[18].

The battery Captain came up this morning and took photographs of the Sgts at this station, and then bought us a beer each, by which time it was "grub up", so we returned to our dining room, which is still in the open. Thank heaven it has not rained at mealtime yet, otherwise we should have got pretty wet. This life of open air is certainly very agreeable, and to get indoors anywhere as we did in Gloucester the other evening gives me that ghastly sleepy headache. It will be a blow to be back to an indoor billet again – if we ever do. Having had lunch we are all now resting. The grub is still small, and I must say that I still feel very hungry. To look at us you would not think we were suffering at all. I have never seen people looking so well. For my part, I am almost like a Red Indian on my face and arms. The old nose is peeling

---

[17] Army colloquialism for ammunition.

[18] A later note added by John on this letter reports that the battery was credited with bringing down a German aircraft, this apparently later being corrected to being a Spitfire. This may, however, refer to the engagement on 25 July by both 281 and 282 batteries of, firstly, a Junkers 88 that was last seen in a shallow dive emitting black smoke, and subsequently a second enemy aircraft that was observed in a vertical spin pursued by two Hurricanes, one of which was later reported to have crashed.

fast. I know you'd be cross as I keep having a tug at a loose piece of skin here and there.

Re. the washing, they have made facilities to get it done down here for us. So I am taking the opportunity of getting it done as I feel postage would be a problem.

Can think of no more news now. Please take care of yourself and write soon if you've time. Until I write again,

Ever your own,

Johnnie.

---

10 July – 11 August 1940
Channel battles.

Gloucester[19], 7 August 1940

Sweetheart darling,

I'm rather afraid that the good habit I had got into seems to have broken down. I don't seem to have been writing nearly so often or such long letters lately, but do so hope you understand dear. As a rule you know that I write you between the hours of two and four in the afternoon, which is our rest period. Somehow or other there always seems to be something that wants doing during this time. At the moment and for the last day or two, Joe Everett, another we've christened 'the eagle' (because he looks so like an eagle), and myself have been put to work to make the Entrance to the camp look more imposing. The work on hand today is a gate which looks rather like some frontier barrier. The finished effect is very good. All painted black and white. The cross bar is only held in place with a catch which when released allows it to raise itself by a heavy drum of concrete on the end.

---

[19] John's Troop moved from Haydons Elm to gun site A15, Parton, 12 July.

We are also building sentry boxes from sandbags. This is my speciality, and I have been complimented for the way they are being done. A scheme is also in hand for chains to be painted white and draped between posts outside the guardroom together with masses of white

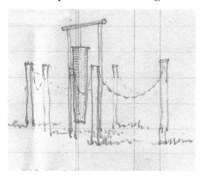

fire buckets. The chains are to make an enclosure to contain the first shell that we fired, suspended from a framework, which we are using as a dinner gong. The shell has been lovingly polished and has a most glorious note when struck. Really looks good. Have just been told we have to go thro' a gas chamber. Will finish when I get back.

Have just returned, and the eyes are just beginning to settle down a bit. It was just ordinary tear gas.

At the moment I am writing sitting in the sun with only a pair of slips on. First bit of sun bathing I have done for ages. Went to the baths yesterday. Had a shower and a swim. You will be very pleased to hear that my hair is getting lighter. I have had it cut short, which you will not like, and am now able to wash it every day. The sun has helped a lot. Hope the weather is like this for our next seven days leave. We shall be able to do some sunbathing. We must also go swimming, for old times sake. Twenty three more days and we shall be together again. It still seems a long way off, but the time is passing quickly.

The news here is very scarce. Have only tomorrow evening, then I shall have finished the sentence[20].

Well dear, must close now to catch post. Very scrappy letter I'm afraid, but people keep talking in the middle of it. I still love you more than I can say. Practical demonstration on Aug 30th!!!!!!

All my fondest love dear, ever your own,

Johnnie.

---

12 August – 23 August
'Eagle Attack', the Luftwaffe's early assault on coastal airfields.

24 August – 6 September
Luftwaffe targets British airfields.

7 September onwards
Daytime attacks switch to British towns and cities, beginning the 'Blitz', that lasted until 21 May 1941[21].

13 September
Italy invades Egypt.

17 September
Hitler abandons 'Operation Sea Lion', the proposed invasion of Britain.

---

[20] John notes against this letter that he was caught asleep whilst on duty, and was accordingly 'sentenced'.
[21] From 7 September, London was bombed fifty-seven nights in succession.

Ever your own, Johnnie, Britain, 1938-42

Weybourne, 2 November 1940[22]

Sweetest darling wife,

It is a terribly happy and excited husband you have writing to you tonight. He's so thrilled he can hardly hold it together. Maybe you will be less excited about it, but to me, and all of us for that matter, it's been the most marvellous thing that has happened. We had a shoot today – that is A section (composed of two subsections – NOT being instruments and No. 2 guns). We started firing at about 09.30 and did not finish until about an hour afterwards. During this time we put up about sixty rounds and brought two "sleeves" (targets) down. It doesn't sound much, I know, being one sleeve for every thirty rounds, but don't forget that the sleeve, being made of cloth, can still be towed even though badly damaged. What really makes me thrilled is that the best shot of all was put up by the gun team that I have been taking such pains training. You've no idea what it did to me to see those eleven men working that gun and bring the sleeve down and then to think that I had been responsible for their training. Just a couple of months ago they were ordinary civilians, and tonight they are experienced gunners and are thrilled. What makes things so much better is the fact that I was not being No. 1 when they did their good work and was only holding a roving commission, giving little tips here and there. They have at last lost all their "gun-shyness" and honestly worked as if they were real old hands at the job.

It's always the done thing that the sleeve is brought back over the gun site and dropped from the plane after the shoot. I've seen lots of sleeves shot down over the sea with yards of cable attached. That's bad shooting. But when you see it disappear in mid air and then the pilot flies back over the gun site to see all that's left are a few shreds of cloth, it's considered damn good shooting. But on top of that we scored over 50% bulls, and 62% effectives. Supposed to be the best

---

[22] John was posted from 88th H.A.A. Regt to 205 A.A. Training Regiment on 15 August, and subsequently at Arborfield Garrison to 349/76th H.A.A. Regt, R.A., on 15 September 1940, being promoted to Sergeant on the same date. 349 Battery had previously been 'thrown off' as a cadre battery from 76th H.A.A. Regt to 207 Training Regiment at Arborfield in early June 1940.

effort down here yet. Imagine how bucked we were! 'Fraid Jerry will
have no chance when we're about. Shooting's by far the best we've
seen. Got 282[23] knocked cold. Am sending you a piece of the first
sleeve. Thought you might be interested. It's about all that was left.
The black mark must be the mark of a shell splinter.

And how's my darling tonight? Been no letter today, but still had one
yesterday, so mustn't be too greedy. Do so wish you were here tonight
dear. I feel so sad and lonely all these miles away from you. If they
would only give some leave soon. Still no more definite news of
movements as to where we are going. Well sweet, no more today –
more tomorrow.

Your adoring husband,

Johnnie.

Sunday 3.11.40 Well gorgeous I missed the post I normally catch in
the mornings. Feel awfully cross about it as it's spoilt my record of a
letter a day. As you will see I had the letter written, but just did not get
time to put it in the post, so thought I would carry straight on with
today's letter on last night's.

After I had written last night we all went over to the camp hall where
there was played upon the stage a variety performance. Gosh! It was
flat as anything. I've never seen a worse show. Fortunately it was all
buckshee. A fat blonde wench was supposed to have been in the Folies
Bergère. Ugh! Revolting. She wore a tight black dress which showed
every bulge of her fat, the skirt being split up the back, showing a
couple of fat legs and a fatter bottom. You know Pegs that sort of
thing does not appeal to me. When she sang songs she had quite a nice
voice – when she did not forget the words! One point in the song she
completely forgot them, and after a few ghastly moments of silence
someone at the back of the hall took up the song for her, and sang
well, with all the words taped off too. She seemed a bit rattled, and
after what she imagined to be a glamorous entrance in the dress she
must have assumed would knock the boys cold, made a very hurried
exit followed by one or two raspberries and catcalls from the boys, and

---

[23] John's former battery in 88th H.A.A. Regt.

a final glimpse of a very fat bottom through an apparently torn dress. Left a nasty taste in my mouth. So cheap and nasty.

The wind made matters worse, and increased to gale force during the performance. Of course, practically the entire cast of "well known artists and artistes" had very weak voices and could not be heard above the roar of the wind. When it blows down here it really means it. Our little bunk faces right into the wind, and all night I could hear the creaking and groaning of timber and the clanking of corrugated iron, and the monotonous bang-banging of a window not properly secured on its catch. Then it rained and in between the roars and whistling of the wind the rain gushed out of a drain and into a gulley just outside my window. It would have been a wonderful opportunity for recording sound effects. There was almost every noise needed for a storm.

We had reveille put forward to 07.00hrs today which meant that the Sgts did not leave bed clothes until 08.00, or rather would not have done so had it not been for the fact that I suddenly found that "A" Sectn had to be digging at 09.00 hrs. Of course I cursed under my heavy moustache and gnashing my teeth swept off to get them off it (it being the day after Saturday here). But when I returned no sign of my flock. I then discovered that the other three sections of the Bty were supposed to be firing and that we had to take over their duties for them. I was told to send the remainder off on a digging squad. So I cast round and found I had one man left over, so I fell him in in three ranks and dismissed him. It's hopeless though. You don't get a chance to keep touch with them.

Geoff is the Battery Orderly Sgt today and getting up earlier than Jackie and I, and as he had to call in at the cookhouse before we were up, he brought us a cup of tea in bed. Gorge! Real luxury these days. After breakfast a hurried chase round for barrack room inspection. Jackie and I went down to the gun park and spent almost the entire morning watching the firing. For our battery it was definitely a failure, and not up to the normal standards. They brought down another sleeve today, but I've a nasty feeling there was about 20 ft. of cable on it. The drill was definitely ragged.

Lunch was the next item on the programme, and after one or two odds and ends here I am writing to my wife, sitting on my blankets in my bunk. Geoff has just come in and at the moment is doing a little sewing. He throws a pretty needle. Most capable type of bloke, and exceptionally clever. Can turn his hand to almost anything, and his knowledge is more like Britannica Encyclopaedia - or do I mean the other way round.

We go back on duty today, and I suppose will not get another free evening until we leave, which as far as I know is next weekend. Corning is giving beers all round to the section tonight for their magnificent shoot yesterday. He's a nice little boy, and we get on very well with him. It's funny to have a section officer of only 22. But still, he knows his drill.

I'm so glad I started this regular letter writing, and do so hope you find these letters as interesting to read as I do to write them. Your letters these days are angelic. So lovely to hear the little intimate thoughts. Will send more tomorrow,

Ever your own, Johnnie.

Weybourne, 6 November 1940

My own darling sweetheart,

Very many thanks for the letter dear which was posted yesterday morning and which arrived this evening. It is grand to get such frequent letters. More like before blitz post. How I ever allowed myself in the past to do anything else other than daily letters I really do not know, and when I think that sometimes I only wrote perhaps once a week or perhaps even less I shudder. But then I did so many things differently in those days. Must go and change the sentries over. Back in a minute.

XXXX.....Brrrrrr!! Dashed cool outside tonight. The old wind seems to be doing its worst. Dashing hither and thither. Just can't seem to keep itself still. It's pitch black outside and you can hear the sound of the breakers on the beach quite clearly up here nearly 400 yds from the shore. I told you last night that I would most likely be on guard tonight. Feels quite strange to be on guard with Gnrs I know. Most of them are members of my gun team, and all are members of the same section. At Arborfield they were all strangers to me. These lads are all jolly good fun. One of the team, 'Nobby' Clarkson, is the most typical cockney I've ever met. He's magnificent. The humour is very dry indeed. Everything he says is funny. I may be stupid, but I can't help laughing at the way he talks. His face does not move a muscle, whether he is serious or pulling someone's leg – which is most of the time. He's the one who uses so many cockney slang terms I was telling you about. Keeping me in fits at the moment.

They've got some tinned salmon. It's not exactly exciting. He's got a piece of what he calls 'ned' (bread). It must measure a foot by nine inches and the salmon is spread about one inch thick. If you could only see it. But not our Nob – eats anything and enjoys it. As he takes a bite (face absolutely expressionless) everyone giggles. All our Nob does is shake his old shaggy head and says, "Makes a change yer know. Nice, to, get, a, bit, o', fish." Do wish you were here. I've had to stop writing several times because I've been laughing so much. Just like a comic show. He's now lying down on his bed with his tin hat over his face after having had a little argument with the bed and the guardroom cat. He might have been talking to anybody – this poor little cat just sat and looked at him very innocently – my sides ache. So good to give them a rest. Well, must post two more sentries. Shan't be long – wind's howling like mad outside. Sounds like a train going by from inside here.

Later. Beautiful night outside. Thousands of stars against a blue black background. The wind is very cold and dry and after all the day's rain the one or two puddles make sparkles here and there, reflecting the silver stars above. As I changed the sentries in the dead still of the night (it's just a few minutes after 02.00hrs) there were a few scurryings of one or two whirls of leaves racing down the road, with the mournful cry of an owl in the lofty elms that creaked and groaned in the sighing wind. They tower over the back of the guard room like huge black sentinels, the only relief against the dark sky in this very flat land – save perhaps for the silhouettes of the huts with their long chimneys, still giving out a red gold spark here and there, and a ragged smudge of black smoke. As the old sentries returned to the guard room I remained for a few minutes looking up into the heavens and offered up a little prayer for a darling by the name of Peggy. Thank you dear God for the blessings of so adorable a wife.

It's been a beast of a day here today – wind and rain – rain and wind. We were to shoot today but the cloud ceiling was so low we could do nothing at all. It is annoying. The other battery have practically finished their ammo and we've hardly started ours. They've had wonderful weather, they really have, and as you can see from ours it's been lousy.

Incidentally, if your Pop gets a spare second or two any time (I don't expect he will) but if he does do you think he could make me a little article as detailed on the next page? I'll explain what it's for, might make it clearer. It's what is called in Artillery a Gauge Protrusion Striker. We use it to gauge the amount the firing pin protrudes clear of the breach. If you look at the diagram you'll see one is .115" and the other .095". The firing pin should touch the .095", and just touch only. The .115" should clear it. When you are firing, as No. 1 of gun, you have to keep checking this to make sure the shell cartridge case is being struck properly. If Pop doesn't have the time don't worry him. I know that he's most likely very busy, and I shall understand. Actually it's a piece of equipment we always for some unknown reason have a very limited supply of and they are hard to come by. They are usually made of metal about $^1/32$" thick. Am sending details just in case. If you think it's rather saucy on my part, don't bother please[24].

The advanced party move off tomorrow, or rather today. Wonder what it will be like there. I now hear that the other Battery is going to where we were!!!! Isn't it extraordinary? NO. Well Pegs, I don't think it will be long now with Roosevelt in do you? They'll most likely be in with men, although we can certainly do with their machines. Won't it be grand to be back in civvies again for good! And then it'll be Mr & Mrs Kemp. Sounds so much better that Sgt & Mrs Kemp somehow.

Well dearest angel heart, I really think that's about all for the time being at least. Hope to write more later today. This letter brings your own adoring husband's fondest love, kisses and cuddles,

Ever your own,

Johnnie.

---

[24] No drawing is present with the letter, so it is assumed that this was passed to Peggy's father, and toolmaker, to make the requested part.

John Kemp's 46th H.A.A. Bristol Brigade badge.

Military Hutments, Woodlands Lane, Almondsbury.

25 November 1940[25]

Peggy my darling,

The new address is as above, but for how long I don't know. Some say only a week. All this time we've been longing for guns. At last we've got them.

We got our movement orders about midday yesterday, and we were here within two hours of receiving the order to move, and within half an hour of arriving, it started. Honestly, we pumped up round after round, and from all accounts it was very accurate. Never before in all my life have I seen anything like it. I haven't been to sleep since yesterday morning, which is now 36 hrs ago. Jerry made a real job of it last night. Incendiaries, H.E., and flares. I leave you to guess the aiming

---

[25] 349 Battery completed training at Weybourne 11 November 1940. It was initially deployed at Hanham as part of 76th H.A.A. Regt. and 46th H.A.A. Brigade, before being ordered to Almondsbury.

point and also what sort of state it's in[26]. 'Fraid we shall have to forget about you coming down here for a while. Digs are impossible to find even if I could get out.

I hear that the old gun site we came from has had a real bashing, but fortunately no casualties. The casualties in the affair last night might have been horrible in numbers on the objective. This gun site is the worst I've seen for mud and comfort.

Oh Pegs, why couldn't your telegram have come a week earlier. How long would you have been able to come for? It's left me in an awfully miserable state. Still, I wouldn't have you here on another night like last night for anything in the world. Maybe you have seen a lot dear, but I still feel last night would have shaken you. I must say it's grand to be able to do something about it instead of just watching.

Have tried to write this in between alarms. Since starting we have put up more rounds and I think there are more to come, so will get some sleep while I can. The old eyes are very heavy. Will write more details tomorrow dear. Do hope you got my telegram.

Ever your own sweetheart,

Johnnie.

349 HAA Battery RA 76th Regt,
Henbury Golf Club, Henbury, Nr Bristol.
29 November 1940

My own darling sweetheart,

Thought I'd make a start to today's epistle before we get called out. It will be a snorter this evening. At the moment I'm sitting in our

---

[26] 148 aircraft bombed Bristol on the night of 24 November 1940, 135 of which attacked between 18.30 and 23.00 hrs, dropping 150 tons of high explosive bombs, 5 tons of oil bombs, and 12,500 incendiaries. The 'Aiming Point' was the docks and nearby industrial premises, the intention being to destroy Bristol and its ability to supply the Midlands and South of England.

hut – which has a fire – it's perishing cold. Heaven knows how the draught manages to find its way in. We have one consolation tonight, in that we have been issued with leather jackets again. They certainly take a lot of beating for warmth. As far as the weather has been concerned it's been a wonderful day. Although there has been a touch of autumn in the air – perhaps a definite tinge of winter – it has been most bracing. I have only one grouse about it and that is a cloudless sky. And it doesn't look like clouding over tonight.

Activity in the air sounds quite considerable. Suppose they must be ours otherwise we should be out already. I can think of many places I'd rather be than standing out in that gun site tonight for hours on end. Admittedly we do have occasional breaks in which we act like a swarm of rabbits and hide ourselves in the dug out at the side of the gun pit which cannot be more than four feet high at its highest point. The roof is corrugated iron and has the most unfortunate habit when we all get in there together of forming little globules of condensation on it and which very rudely drop down one's neck as the old head nods off to sleep. One of the lads, as I believe I told you, stops to bring a hurricane lamp up with him. It does make it seem a bit more cheerful. I hate to think what it would have been like last night had it not been for Nobby Clarkson and his mates wisecracking. I do wish you could have the chance of coming out with us one evening and just hearing the conversation. It's going to be a yell after this "business" is over bumping into these lads. But it's going to take a long time to forget last night's standing by and watching all those planes going over one after the other at regular intervals with absolutely nothing to stop them. Every single one of them out of range for us. Just couldn't get anywhere near them. Heaven knows, it was cold enough on the ground, what it must have been like at that height I just hate to think, but still they came. Where they went I don't know, but I do know that we were still here when they came back. There was just one thing that absolutely beat me last night, and that was one single gun position that would fire shells that burst right over our heads. Can't think where the guns were but they certainly made an extraordinary noise. It wasn't the noise we objected to so much as the untidy habit of pieces of shell and fuse cap dropping all over the place several minutes after the shell had burst. I'm told that this was happening all the time during the Battle of Bristol on Sunday night, but I must confess I didn't hear them. Last night for the first time I had the experience of hearing portions of shell whistling through the air. It was more of a hum ended by a plop as the pieces hit the mud. One piece sounded uncomfortably near. We found several jagged edges round the guns today. Still, I expect this is all a daily occurrence for you. No sirens yet, or whistles, expect they are just being damned cussed – most likely over later – when it's colder!

Well my sweetest angel, no more news now. I'm sending you the new address of B.H.Q. I think it will be better to address all letters to this in future, as we shall apparently be switching about a hell of a lot. Did I tell you I think we shall be returning to Hanham this weekend for a week, then back here again, unless of course they decide to send us to some other gun site equally far from civilisation. This site must be miles and miles away from the nearest human being. The only person I've seen looking like a real human was a land girl in the field next door.

Well my twenty carat sweetheart, all the love in the world, and especially your husband's fondest adoration kisses.

Ever your very own,

Johnnie.

Military Hutments, Woodlands Lane, Almondsbury.

10 December 1940

My own darling Sweetheart,

With all my heart dearest and everything I can summon, let me thank you for everything you did to help make such a wonderful seven days. Darling, I shall always remember it. There are so many little incidents that will always make it stand out in my memory as seven days of heaven. All the little things you did for me angel heart I shall never be able to let you know the depth of my appreciation. This is the first leave I can remember returning from that I really feel has done me good. If you can say that you have enjoyed it for only half as much, I can rest thankful that it was the most enjoyable you have ever had. My most angelic sweetheart from the bottom of my poor little heart that aches so much for you, thank you darling angel.

The journey back was straightforward and uneventful. I arrived at Paddington at 15.15hrs, and consequently had an hour's wait for the train that went out punctually at 16.15hrs as scheduled. I met Ken on Paddington and we travelled down together and had quite an enjoyable journey, although rather long and tedious. We could not get right into the centre of the city station - I suppose as a result of last week's air raids – and had to alight at a station outside, which was actually nearer the camp. Incidentally, please note the above address – I should write here until further notice as I now understand we shall be here for at least a month. Now for some real good news, sit back, make yourself comfortable, turn your ears back and listen. I have it on very good authority that a new system has or is about to be inaugurated whereby we shall have 48hrs leave each month, 24hrs leave each week (which I shall not bother about), and seven days every three months. Can you imagine any better news to come back to. It has put such a different light on the whole affair. At the moment, until it becomes a confirmed statement, I shall view it as only provisional. What a difference it will make to be able to see you once a month. It's made a new man of me. Especially as it came practically at the same time as the news of our offensive against the 'wops' – I bet Pop is feeling a little better tonight. I wouldn't mind a gin and It myself if I were there tonight.

Do so hope things are quiet tonight. Suppose you are on duty now. Bless you my dearest darling. Apparently last week down here was one big crash. Have not seen much of it, but there is certainly a deuce of a lot of wreckage about the place. Curse 'em. But we'll beat 'em yet.

This is only short dearest, as I've a lot of sorting out to do tonight, and get everything just where I want it in case we have any "fun". It's now 20.45hrs and so far it's been very quiet. Only one alarm that came to nothing. Will write again tomorrow, dear, and take care of the sweetest wife in the world for me. Your husband has said how much he enjoyed his leave, and how grateful he is,

Ever your adoring husband,

Johnnie.

Ever your own, Johnnie, Britain, 1938-42

pen and ink sketch by John Kemp of the Bristol Mess, Christmas 1940

1941

349 H.A.A. B⁺ʸ, 76ᵗʰ Reg⁺ R.A.
Memorial Road Gun Site,
Hanham, Near Bristol,
Gloucestershire.

(*Friday, January 10ᵗʰ 1941.*)

My own darling Mrs Sgt Kemp,

Another letter today. This time to the correct address. Thank you my sweetheart. So lovely to the old regularity.

Geoff has just come in saying it's definitely on the cards that this half battery is on the move again very shortly to another site. Still in this locality. Can't give you any more details yet. Hope it won't mess the 48hrs up! I know no other details yet. You can still write here till we get the line up on it.

The coffee table sounds gorge dear. Sorry about the tallboy. Do you think it's absolutely impossible to store it anywhere? It strikes me it might be a good idea to get hold of these sorts of things now. I've a rather nasty feeling these sorts of things are going to be very expensive after the war. Still, I'll leave it to you dearest.

Glad you like the sketch. Have done another of the interior of the mess, but am rather proud of this one and do not want to send it for fear of creasing it, so will let you have it on next leave. Hope to do some more. Hope you like it.

Was very sorry to hear about Gran, do so hope it is not too bad. Give her my love when you see her next and tell her I hope she will soon be better.

Quite a lot of activity here last night, but no "pennies from heaven". Had a little action late this afternoon, think it was just reconnaissance. Firing was quite good. First daylight action in this battery. I haven't been manning today, and have tonight off so it means pyjamas tonight. Will be quite a change to go out in a crowd tonight.

News is very scarce tonight dear. Except of course the much repeated I love you.

Ever your very own husband,

Johnnie.

Hanham, Friday 24 January 1941

My own darlingest wife,

I feel that I always write to thank you after a leave, thanking you so profusely for all you do for me when I am at home and for the wonderful time you give me. If I could only think of some different and more impressive way of expressing my gratitude for the last leave I would do so. But all I can say is thank you dear, it was sheer heaven - every little bit of it.

Having left Mother at E.Croydon I went down onto the platform and met Paddy Lake of 282. He's home on seven days, and was going up to see his lady friend. From all accounts I have been lucky to get out of it when I did. Things don't sound too happy.

We caught a train almost immediately. Actually, I was very lucky in the trains. I caught a train at Victoria underground almost immediately I got on the platform. The windows in the underground are covered with that netting, and make it very difficult to see the stations. Consequently every time the train stops hoards of people jump up and rush to the doors to look out. The train stopped on one occasion in between station, and an old dear jumped up and in spite of the fact that she was told it wasn't a station opened the door, and had the train not started suddenly, she would have taken a purler out of the door. Without further interest I duly arrived at Paddington to find the train waiting for me. Had a good window seat with very uninteresting travelling companions. One was apparently a managing director or something like that, and he smoked a very long and evil smelling cigar. Am enclosing impressions of the people in the compartment.

Sketches by John Kemp of his travelling companions, included in the letter.

The rake smoked cigarettes incessantly, while the old boy next to me slept and snored very vigorously in between a series of convulsive jumps, about which he seemed rather embarrassed, as he kept staring round to see if anyone had noticed. The man opposite was "seen off" by a very gutsy wench who was "fraightfully" worried about his Enormous Case which was perched very precariously on the rack over his head. He entered the train with a miniature bookstall. He'd practically every evening and daily paper and also "Lilliputs", "Picture Post" etc., and only just glanced through them though, then eventually settled down to read the Daily Mirror which he read from start to finish, and all the time I was concentrating on nasty garlic and other obnoxious smells.

Arriving at Bristol at 7.55 I could hardly see a thing. It was so black you could feel the darkness. It was in the train coming from the station to Hanham that I decided to ring you, so when I got out I went straight to the phone box, and was told I would have to wait and they'd ring again. I first of all burned my fingers with matches trying to find the number, and ended up dropping them all over the place. Well you know the result. They lost the number and I had to wait. Still, it was grand to get through, and as I said I'll see what I can do next week.

Today has been a day of much shouting. Have been drilling the new lads, and George Bishop and I have had to resort to the old Arborfield Barrack Square methods. George's voice is wicked. Can be heard all over Bristol. And when someone turned right instead of left, that done it! They had P.T. this afternoon. Never seen anything like it. Their legs looked like sticks of forced rhubarb, all straight and white.

Had a pleasant surprise tonight. Found that they had not had the kidneys. We had them for tea today. Most tasty – real relish! I had my hair cut tonight. Know you'll be mad, but will see that I don't have it so short for the next leave.

Well dearest, that's all the news. Ever with adoration and kisses,

All your very own,

Johnnie.

Pencil sketch by John Kemp of Sgt "Nobby" Clarkson,
8 February 1941.

Whitchurch, Monday 10 February 1941

My darling,

I hope this will arrive in time. Am sending it off a little earlier than perhaps necessary so that I can be sure of your receiving it on time. Sorry it isn't in colour. Could have made something out of it. I feel very upset that I was unable to write to you yesterday dearest, but after the day's work, I'd just come back and started on this when the confounded alarm went. No sooner had we been 'stood down' than it went again. The second time proved a little more fruitful, and for the first time these boys have been into action on a 'Camel' equivalent. It was an absolute swine of a night, with a perpetual downpour on both alarms. Made a lot of unnecessary work today. The poor old breech was in a ghastly mess. Still, the boys were thrilled to fire again. It did them good. After we were stood down the second time it must have been near 12 o'clock, and I felt so sleepy and thinking you'd understand if I took a lil sleep, I left your letter till today, and this is the first opportunity. It's been a beautiful day, and the night is perfect. We're on our toes, just waiting. Feel sure we'll be out.

Received your letter today sweetest. Thank you my sweet. I see you're apparently expecting me home on Tue 17th. I don't know if that's the date I gave you. If it was it's wrong, and I should have said 18th, which is a week tomorrow. It'll be heavenly to see you again sweetheart. It's one of my most prominent thoughts at the moment.

Well sweetest heart, no more tonight. Until I come home you'll be ever in my thoughts.

Ever your own,

Johnnie.

P.S. wrote to Tich. It's his birthday on 11th. Said I'd get him something cheap when on leave.

Whitchurch, Sunday 6 April 1941

Darling,

Have a little more time tonight I hope before anything is likely to happen. Thankfully last night it was most peaceful and quiet. It was a great blessing, most welcome. I was very sorry not to be able to give any more details about things, but on both occasions I was very pressed for time. Normally when I write it's always with a feeling of being called out in the middle of it all. Consequently I always rush through it so that it will be ready to post. Last night I did not finish it until well after eight and was expecting to be called out any moment.

We had quite a lot of "fun" on Thursday and Friday. After about five rounds had been fired on Thursday, I caught a terrible blast from the side of the gun, and completely lost my sight and hearing for a good deal of time. It was hopeless to try to do No. 1. So I put a Bdr on as number 1 of the gun, and myself performed duties of an ammunition number. I must say I thoroughly enjoyed it, and by the time we'd finished I was practically stripped and sweating like mad. I think these two nights were the heaviest barrages I've ever seen, and am glad to say it was with very good results. Peg, we had the thrill of seeing a Jerry crash in flames[27]. Wonderful sight it was. I understand that ten planes have been accounted for, and on top of which we turned back many waves of bombers who were forced to drop their bombs at random. There were one or two whistlers which came quite close, and a stick of incendiaries dropped uncomfortably near. Still, no damage was caused. I still did ammo on Friday as the ears were not quite right. They are quite alright now, and I was a fool I suppose not to wear plugs.

Most of the time these last few days – as you can imagine – has been very occupied with carrying ammo into the gun pits – and that is as far

---

[27] The only record of German aircraft being brought down on 3rd/4th April 1941, and 4th/5th April 1941 are credited to night fighter action. That on 3rd/4th was a Junkers Ju 88A-5, Wnr.4224, V4+AR of 7/KG1, credited to a Beaufighter of 604 Sqdn, crashing near the Needles, Isle of Wight. That on 4th/5th was Heinkel He 111 H-5, Wnr. 3595, 1H+ED of Stab.III/KG26, also credited to a Beaufighter of 604 Sqdn, crashing at Reading's Farm, Hewish, Near Weston-Super-Mare.

as I can see – unless anything goes wrong, - is the last time I shall do No. 1 on a Gun. From tomorrow I am being transferred to B.H.Q. staff. I think I am now in a position to explain all the mystery I portrayed in an earlier letter, but darling please don't mention this to Mother and Father just yet. If I am successful in my work, darling, I shall realise one of my dreams, and I know it's one of yours too. The B.S.M. is leaving the Bty for a position in R.H.Q. so I have been told that I have to go over and study his job. So unless I come unstuck there's a little more promotion in the near future. But dearest, please say absolutely nothing to anyone at home. Not until I manage to carry it off. I really don't know quite how to feel about it all. Apart from the fact that I've got to start from scratch, I feel I'm only a kid to take the job on. Still, it's the chance I've been waiting for, and I'm going absolutely all out for it. There's going to be real work to do from now onwards. I'm still in a whirl about it all, and cannot appreciate the position. It's just too good to be true. If it does come off, it will mean 10/- a day!!! And an extra allowance for you. So hold me back! Now, please dearest, don't forget, say nothing about it to anyone until it's through. It will be nicer to wait until it's definite. So don't tell anyone even if it's in confidence!! as it's rather hush this end. You'd better be careful what you say in your letters just in case someone should find it. And regards leave, I don't know what will happen now. I shall have to fall in with their rota now over at B.H.Q. and am very afraid that I shall not be able to have much time off for quite a while as there's so much to be learned. Still, I'll let you know more details when I get stuck in. So sorry sweet, but this is a wonderful chance for both of us. And that about finishes my news tonight. Feel it's the best I've ever been able to give you.

More tomorrow darling heart,

Ever your own husband's love and adoration,

Johnnie.

---

11 April 1941
Axis forces begin Siege of Allies in Tobruk.

349th Bty, H.A.A. Battery R.A., Whitchurch, 10 May 1941

Peggy Darling,

You must be thinking me most awful mean with all this lack of writing lately, but things seem to have to spoil all my usual arrangements. Last night I was most earnest about going straight back from the office and writing you a real long letter, only to find that at 7.30 I was supposed to be playing in the darts team against the locals down the pub. Very kindly they had made all arrangements for me, and when I protested, I was told that one Sgt must go, and that I had been detailed for it, which I found most annoying. So as things are quiet in the office this afternoon I'm taking this opportunity of writing you darling.

I had a parcel from you this afternoon just as I was leaving the mess. Thank you darling. I just can't believe it. My wife making me cookies and sending them to me. It is so sweet of you dearest.

I feel I ought to give you a little news. I've done so little lately. The last time I wrote you I said I heard a rather suspicious plane overhead. I'd no sooner sealed the envelope down than the alarm went, and another night out there until 05.30hrs. Last night was the first night we've been in bed before 2 o'clock for well over a week, and for most of the boys it must be nearly a fortnight. We have not had that much activity here really. Plenty of planes going over, working in conjunction with the R.A.F. we have been accounting for quite a number of "his" planes. I'm rather out of date with the news I have given lately, so if some of it's rather stale please forgive me. I believe I told you that we have had several planes down round here, two of which during the last week, we have seen come down in flames[28]. Great sight.

The night referred to on the wireless as a raid on the Bristol Channel area was not so very bad, or at least I've seen worse. There were large numbers of fires which were in two cases very sad. I believe I told you about that though. I saw it through the telescope, and watched house after house fall down into the furnace. Last night we were called out at

---

[28] Records indicate that a Heinkel He 111, 1G+NA, was shot down by a Beaufighter of 600 Sqdn on the night of 7/8 May.

23.30 until 07.30. Did not fire a shot, and even though there were one or two planes about we stood down. The long night's sleep made me feel more tired than when we're out all night.

Thank you for the list of times for phoning dearest, I hope to be able to ring you up tomorrow evening.

I've been plodding away in the office all this week. Nothing unusual has happened in this sphere, and I'm still waiting further in the direction we're both anxious about.

I was very thrilled with the pipe Tich and Ruth sent. I was very impressed with the selection. It shows I've trained my kid brother well, as it has everything I could ask for in a pipe.

As no doubt you will have noticed, I have been able to write all of this in the office. I seemed no sooner to have started when work just showered in. And the time now is exactly 23hrs by Big Ben, and very nearly zero hour. Feel very cross as I'd meant to write so much today, but seem always to be prevented. Well I'm damned, in the middle of Big Ben the sirens went. We thought it was here and immediately rushed. Turned off the wireless only to find it was on the wireless.

Oh darling, I do hope they leave you alone tonight. Makes me feel worried. Suppose ours will be going soon, and I'd better go so that this will catch the first post tomorrow morning.

All fondest love and adoration darling,

Ever your own lover and husband,

Johnnie.

Whitchurch, Sunday 18 May 1941

My Darling,

I'm so sorry that I didn't write yesterday dear. I had every intention of doing so, but after a very busy day in the office, I got back to camp in the evening to find there was a dance being held. Actually, I knew that they were going to hold one, but had no idea that there was going to be a party in the mess as well.

It was only a glorified stag party, no females being allowed into our mess. I suppose that I was not back much before 19.00hrs and it was just about getting into its swing by then. After I had had my tea and a wash it was getting well into the evening, and absolutely impossible to write a letter what with everyone using their vocal organs to the fullest extent. Added to which there was also this dance going on in the canteen next door, so I thought I'd put your letter off until the riot had subsided a little, but that was just where I was wrong because it must have been about 02.00hrs before we eventually got to bed. I'm very sorry dearest, and do so hope you will understand, as it's the last thing I want to do to make you wait for a letter.

The party we had in the mess was quite a good affair and developed into a whist school half way through. I was never meant to be a card player, although I enjoyed it very much. The dance itself was a great success I gather from the reports I have received from the boys. I only had a look in for about half an hour. I suppose that I went at the wrong time really. Unless you've been there all the time you can't really appreciate it properly. To me it looked just like a seething mass of humanity, very few of whom gave me the impression they knew how to dance. I had a couple of attempts to keep off some very typical west country wench's foot, without much success. I admit I'm no Fred Astaire. But my main fault is that I will never be able to enjoy a dance unless my Peggy is there with me.

I am so looking forward to seeing you again. It is a great pity that you are unable to arrange your leave for 10th. I know you told me you were asking for the last week in June, but was rather under the impression that this was only tentative. The rest of your Post[29] have been very kind to us and as you say they ought to have a little consideration some times. I think I should be able to adjust my leave to fit in with yours, but until I hear a definite date from you dear I'll keep it open.

I had hoped that there would be a chance of ringing you up last night, but was told that they are still only accepting priority calls still, so I

---

[29] A.R.P. ambulance post.

expect that that will mean that there is no chance of my being able to get through to you on the telephone for quite a while now. It is a nuisance, as the telephone was just beginning to be really helpful, and it is so heavenly to hear your sweet voice, even if it only for three minutes a week.

I went down to the Hippodrome, as I said I was intending, on Friday evening with Jackie Cooper. It really was a first class show. It was the first time that I had seen Duggie Wakefield. If you have not, I strongly recommend you take the chance if you should get one.

I don't think there is any more news dearest. We have been out once since I last wrote, but there was nothing much at all in our range. They were going up North I should imagine, and I only fired three rounds having stood out there from 23.30hrs until 04.00hrs. It really is most annoying.

All my very fondest love and adorations darling heart,

All your very own husband,

Johnnie.

---

20 May 1941
German Forces invade Crete.

31 May 1941
British Forces surrender in Crete.

---

103 Wharnecliffe Gardens, Wells Road, Bristol 4.
Sunday 8 June 1941

My very dearest wife,

I was very sorry to hear such a sad girl on the phone last night. I must agree that the settling of this leave has all been annoying and to say the least unsatisfactory. I must appear most unreasonable and thoughtless in all I do over these sort of things. Dear Sweetheart, for all inconvenience caused to you and anyone else, please accept and believe that the handling of it has been completely out of my hands, and I feel so very upset and sad about it all. Poor darling, you did sound so very depressed. But I can promise you that this leave question was not my doing, although I believe you feel just a little sore with me for it. Still, I'll see what can be done to get leave as near the 19th as possible. As we cannot travel at weekends for seven days leave it will have to be 20th or 23rd now. As I told you Roberts and the O.C. go to camp at the end of next week, and will consequently not be back before 23rd. I expect he will let me go on 20th. The only trouble is that my going then will leave no Sgt at B.H.Q., which is a little awkward. I'll let you know all about it on the phone next week dear.

I've had a very lazy day today, and spent it all in bed as I had a very sleepless night. This inoculation is an awful nuisance. It is not so bad as last year's dose, but the rotten part is the M.O. jabbed both arms. Last time it was left arm only, and that means you can sleep on your right side, but now it's only possible to sleep on the back, and I got a little muddled last night when I was half asleep and couldn't make out why I couldn't sleep on my left or right side.

Incidentally, you will see a different address on this letter. I have now moved from the gun site, and am rooming with "Taffy" Evans, the Q. bloke, in a semi-detached house of very poor construction and quality. Still, we are quite comfortable in our little room. We have a wireless set, and best of all, a batman. Great treat, and saves a lot of time in the mornings as he cleans boots and brass as well as getting washing and shaving water.

I do hope that I shall hear some more definite news of promotion before I come home - I have a feeling it won't come off until after I come back, in view of the fact that the old man is going away next week. Old Taffy is also awaiting promotion to Quartermaster, and we both feel rather cross to think we are doing jobs without the promotion that goes with it.

I've been very busy these last few days. There has always been plenty to do, and never an end in it all. We (Taffy and I) try to go for a walk down to the local and back about 9.30. It's impossible to try and stay in doors all day, and it makes a little break. The day is really long you know. We start about 9 in the morning, and go on until 9 at night. I had hoped to be able to make this a long letter, but 'fraid I'll have to close as the arms are aching quite a bit. Now, my dearest darling, for tonight all my fondest love and kisses to the sweetest girlie in the world,

from her own,

Johnnie.

Pencil sketch of Jackie "Taff" Evans, by John Kemp

103 Wharncliffe Gardens, Wells Road, Bristol 4.
Tuesday 10 June 1941

Most wonderful wife in The World,

For a terribly sweet letter this morning my sincerest thanks
dear heart. I had worked so very hard all day yesterday hoping I would
get all finished and have time to write to you last night. I eventually
downed tools just before 12, and felt so thoroughly whacked that I
crawled straight into bed. I think the inoculation has pulled me down a
lot. Even the O.C. told me I looked tired and said I ought to go to bed.
All very nice on the face of it, but it doesn't work in practise. I <u>had</u> to
get a hundred and one jobs settled before this morning – I have never
seen so much work as I had yesterday and today. I can't think why it is
when I feel well and fit for stacks of work I get nothing, and just
because I've not been feeling quite up to the mark, in it comes wallop.
Still, I've just managed to break the back of it all today. Have only just
finished, and it's just gone midnight, and in my humble opinion time all
little gunners, whether potential B.S.M.s or not, should be abed asleep.
Old "George" [30] is a stickler for work – when he feels inclined. We
might go for a whole week and have nothing at all, and then he
suddenly decides to clear his mail, and it just pours out like a waterfall.
He writes reams and scratches away for miles more paper than we
actually see in his office. I expect the silly old ---- is still over there
wearing his pencil down. But it's not too bad really for him. He has a
reveille of his own round about midday, and ours is still 08.00hrs with
work commencing at 09.00. So we are putting in about 13hrs work a
day. Not too bad, I suppose, but there are times when I think I shall
not reach the end of all I've got to do, and as a result of the delay in a
lot of odds and ends in his office, it has all to be done in a deuce of a
rush. I can tell you I'm getting quite professional with the typewriter. If
only you could see my list of jobs for tomorrow. It's about as long as
this page in much smaller writing than this.

---

[30] "George" was an officer in the regular army. He had, on 21 May 1940, been
posted to 88th H.A.A. Rgt with the rank of Captain, before being promoted
to Major and assuming command of 283/88 Battery. He was subsequently
transferred to 76th H.A.A. Regt as battery commander of 349 Battery.

I have heard nothing about promotion yet, and unfortunately am not in a position to ask him about it. That's the snag of the army. It's not like a civvie job where you can almost demand these sorts of things or perhaps a rise. In the army they're just as likely to remove you altogether. Still, perhaps it's a little early yet, and he has not had time to try me out enough, so I suppose that after all I shall come home minus the crown. It's a damn nuisance, but there it is. I think it will eventually go through. The back pay will be nice!!

I had a letter from old Geoff the other day. Very little news in his letter. Heaven knows what I shall do about answering all these letters now. It's just about as much as I can do to write to the loveliest Girlie in the World, let alone my ex-rivals. Also had another letter from Bob. I owe him one too now. I suppose I'll be able to get to the bottom of it soon. I hope!

I had hoped to phone you tonight, but what good at 12? All my kisses and adorations to you sweet, and please take great care.

Ever your very own,

Johnnie.

103 Wharnecliffe Gardens, Wells Road, Bristol 4.
Wednesday 11 June 1941

Darling Heart,

You really are the sweetest girl ever. How can I thank you for all your dear gifts? Darling, from the bottom of this humble heart, thank you. This paper is swank and gorge to write on[31]. Thank you too for the baccy dear. You are an angel.

I've just discovered that I did not post yesterday's letter. It was a complete oversight. Can't think why. I always give it to the P.R.[32] first thing in the morning with the other mail, but suppose as today has

---

[31] The writing paper is crested with the Royal Artillery insignia.
[32] Post Room.

been such a rush on account of people going to camp tomorrow it was overlooked.

With your registered parcel today I also had one from my Pop enclosing baccy, so I shall be alright for now. Gorge! He tells me Tich is being called up on Saturday week. Goes to Torquay. Must see if I can contact him somehow or other. Old Bob has got himself all tied up in this commission racket. Perhaps you know all this already. Apparently Conduit Street[33] is not too happy, and I gather Pop and Ma are feeling very down. Makes me feel sad when I hear all these things, especially when I've seen all Pop has put into the business. I know it's happening all over the world. Cases even harder than this. But it does go to your heart when it's your family, doesn't it?

It's been a hectic day today. Old George (the O.C.) has felt quite "festive". I think he's quite thrilled at the thought of going to camp[34] tomorrow. I know I'm glad he's going. It will at least give me a little peace to get things straightened out while he's away. But he's a bit of a crank at times and most trying. When he gets these working fits you can reckon you'll be at it and hang the midnight oil. I've come back tonight at 00.30hrs. But there were lots of odds and ends to straighten up, and the potential B.S.M. must have the reins in his hands and his feet in the irons. He's been like a man possessed from 22.00hrs onwards. Yards and yards of paper have been covered and pencils worn down to stumps. I'll bet he's still at it now. Usually works until 03.00hrs, so I'm told. But that's his fault, and after he comes back from camp he'll see me rarely after 21.00hrs.

It's been a glorious day today (the weather, not the work!) and Geoff and I had to go out to our other site[35] this afternoon to check the drills etc. They are under canvas. Very nice and healthy today, but the poor devils roughed it recently in all this rain. They all look very brown in spite of it though. They are in a really beautiful spot miles from anywhere out in the back of beyond. It was so nice to get out for the afternoon, and the countryside did look beautiful. All manner of wild

---

[33] Location of John's father's business.
[34] Practice camp at Bude with composite battery.
[35] During June 1941, 349 Battery was sited at Whitchurch (Bristol 17) adjacent to Wharncliffe Gardens, with 4 static guns, and Chew (Bristol 18), to the south of Bristol, with 4 mobile guns.

flowers in this part of the world, and most beautiful of these was rhododendrons in a great magenta splash up the slope of a hill to a glorious ivy clad house. I do love the country here. It's glorious. I suppose it's been one of the best days this year with really lovely cloud formations. I expected a little fun tonight, but up till now there has been nothing to my knowledge, and suppose it must be about 01.30hrs now. So they're leaving it rather late. Hope it doesn't mean they are anywhere near you dear. Saw Tom Dale out there this afternoon, and George Bishop, both asked after you.

Apart from all the above chatter, I can't think of any more news. I have completely recovered from the inoculation and am now back to normal today.

Well my darling one, I seem to have covered nearly all the last 24hrs, and as I have to be up at 06.00hrs I think I'll turn in. I have a camp party to see off at that unearthly hour.

Take great care,

Ever adoringly with many thanks,

Johnnie.

103 Wharnecliffe Gardens, Wells Road, Bristol 4.
Friday 13 June 1941

My own Darling Sweetheart,

I had another adorable letter yesterday from the Sweetest ever. So sorry to hear that she has a cold. Do hope it's better now dear darling.

In answer to your question, if you write to this address you are always sure of my getting it since I live here as well as working here. That is unless I get the order of the boot. As yet I have heard nothing more, and as mentioned in a previous letter, I expect I shall have to wait until after the leave now. It's a nuisance, but still, just the luck of the game.

Now darling, a snag has arisen in the leave. I hate to tell you that, and I expect your face will drop considerably, but in a way, it will be all to the good. Let me explain. As you know the O.C. and Roberts have gone to camp, and do not return until 24th which rather means that I cannot go until 25th. Now what I was thinking was, how do you like the idea of coming down here on 22nd and then I could see you then and come back with you, perhaps breaking the journey on the way home. I think I could find somewhere to put you up, the only trouble would be that I should not be able to see you all the day, but I could work it that I got the afternoon off on 23rd and on 24th should be able to spend all night with you, perhaps about or after midnight, then go straight home with you on 25th. Let me know what you think of this. I'm afraid it cannot possibly be helped dear and if they must alter the date of the camp it's most annoying. I never remember having a leave mucked about quite so much.

Sorry I did not write last night, but I was so dead at 12 o'clock last night I just couldn't keep my eyes open. I'd been on the go since 5.30 in the morning, having only finished writing to you at 2.30. Incidentally I spoke rather too soon about it being a quiet week down here. I'd no sooner finished writing when the sirens went. I heard one or two planes go over and then dropped off to sleep. Apparently there were two land mines dropped in B. I don't know what damage they did. I did not hear them.

Have been terribly busy today tidying up different little odd jobs George left for me. Was glad to see him go yesterday. He had worked with Roberts all through the night, and when I went in at about 6 there were stacks of notes and typed letters etc. He must be barmy! I have had an evening off tonight, and went to the Hippodrome and saw a very good show with some very sweet little girls. There were twin dancers who had the most beautiful legs I've ever seen with one exception, my wife's!

No more tonight dear, please let me know as soon as poss about this alteration darling.

All my fondest love and kisses dear,

Ever adoringly,

Johnnie.

103 Wharncliffe Gardens, Wells Road, Bristol 4.
Sunday 15 June 1941

My darling Girlie,

Had no letter yesterday, and as today's Sunday I feel a sad little sausage. Still, I expect the reason is that you have been waiting for my letters. Writing to you last night was absolutely out of the question, no matter how much I wanted to do so. There's been another exercise on here all night with hoards of H.G. and other troops. The thing that rather got me beat was staying awake all night. Feel just right for a sleep right now. So wish you were here. Still, only another week now, and I shall be seeing my Peggy. I do hope by some chance that something can be done about the 25th, or failing that that you can come down on 23rd.

Its about 09.30 now, and I'm feeling terribly grumpy and in need of a wash. We have only just returned and had breakfast. Today will be very disorganised as we've started like this.

George came back last night from camp to see the exercise. He is absolutely crackers. Incidentally, he left his revolver (loaded) in a railway carriage. Fine example to set.

As far as I'm concerned I saw nothing of the supposed invasion troops, although I'm given to understand that our site was wiped out. I dozed off for about 10 mins, otherwise I've been right through the clock since 08.00hrs yesterday. I hope to get a very long night in bed tonight, and shall retire somewhere about 18.00hrs, write to my peachy gorge and then sleep till morning.

Well my dearest heart, must of necessity make this letter very short.

Ever your very own adoring husband,

Johnnie.

---

22 June
German Forces commence Operation Barbarossa, the invasion of Soviet Union.

---

103 Wharnecliffe Gardens, Wells Road, Bristol 4.
Thursday 3 July 1941

My darlingest Sweetheart,

I have had a really nice change tonight, and had the evening off. Instead of coming straight back from tea I stayed on in the mess and played 'solo' from 18.30 until 22.00hrs. It was a most welcome rest after the work I've been putting in recently. It was most enjoyable. I won a couple of bob on the evening which helped to make it a little more enjoyable perhaps! I managed to complete all the outstanding stuff last night and I really think George appreciated it, although he said very little so it was with a clear conscience that I took last night's work as a reason for a rest tonight.

There has been very little to do at B.H.Q. I performed my usual morning inspection after breakfast keeping people up to scratch. Most of the day I have had letters to write to site office telling them what to do!!! I feel all a very valuable experience in that light and must confess I do love doing it. I spent this afternoon very easily with quite an interesting job, sorting out Guard Duty at Brigade. It's practically a day's work sorting out the correspondence. What is cancelled and what still stands. Just like the British Army!

I had no letter from you today. Still, I did not deserve it. I suppose I should have been writing to you a longer letter instead of playing cards, and I feel mean over it.

No more tonight dear angel. All fondest love and adoration,

Ever adoringly,

Johnnie.

Ever your own, Johnnie, Britain, 1938-42

103 Wharncliffe Gardens, Wells Road, Bristol 4.
Wednesday 9 July 1941

Dear darling Gorgeous,

Another day gone, and as I write it's just striking 24.00hrs. Wow! The news – Vichy sounds like throwing the old sponge in the ring. That will help us a great deal. Can't understand why they ever started.

Well it's now Thursday really, I suppose, and that only means another week before I see you again. Rather an encouraging thing happened tonight. I was in the O.C.'s office having the usual evening sort out of letters, work, etc., and there was a letter from Brigade, or somewhere 'up above' about leave which we discussed very fully. After we'd discussed it, the old man said "Let me see, you go on leave on 18th don't you?" So of course yours truly said a firm "Yessir." Then Old George said "Will your wife be able to get her leave then?" and I said I didn't think she would. I didn't want to sound too nice and make things as awkward as I could. He wanted to know what your job was and all about it. Thought, as I do, that the Y.M.C.A. work is too much on top of A.R.P. But I thought that this was all a very good sign, especially that he's not forgotten, as I dreaded that he might. So it looks very much like the 18th after all. Can't think why it was cancelled in the first place

I have to go out to our other site tomorrow with the O.C. to try a bloke for drunkenness. Should be quite an enjoyable trip. Have been very busy today clearing up little odd jobs. I'm nearly straight now, so hope to be able to take some more time off.

How's my darling wife tonight – Gosh! I'm longing to see you again sweetheart.

No more tonight.

Ever you very own adoring Johnnie.

103 Wharncliffe Gardens, Wells Road, Bristol 4.
Sunday 27 July 1941[36]

Sweetest Angel in the World,

    In spite of all my hopes and promises that I would phone or write you before this, I have been frustrated by one hundred and one little jobs. On top of which came an exercise last night. The west countryside has teemed with rather odd assortments of Home Guards and very red faced stubbly chinned soldiers for rather a large part of the past 24hrs. It wouldn't have been too bad had it been left at that, but my company was requested. So I sprang very nimbly from chaste couch promptly at 05.00hrs and proceeded to scene of battle to see how we were doing. The situation was just beginning to develop, although still rather vague. A realistic effect was given by some "dive bombers". It certainly gave an idea of what to expect. Just when I arrived a "gas bomb" or two were very carelessly "dropped" by an umpire. So the very heavily clad P.A.D.[37] Squad lumbered into action and carried out decontamination in the vicinity. Very effective. At one point in the proceedings it came to a very smart bit of hand to hand fighting with a very "shot-up" party of Home Guards. Apparently they had previously been wiped out by rifle, machine gun, and 3.7" gun fire, and were not content until they were finally, literally, sat on by one or two of the heavier members of the site. There were quite a lot of heavy blows exchanged until they were eventually told by the umpire that – at last - they must consider themselves dead and gone. They seemed very sad at this, apparently they wanted to be allowed to go on in spite of this.

Since I have been back I have been kept company by the most wonderful dreams of the darling girl who made my leave the most perfect heaven. It does not seem possible after all that waiting I have now had that leave. But still, I have brought back with me the most marvellous memories it is possible for any man living to have. Never in all my life have I been so lucky as I was on that day I met you. Dear darling, I love you so much, and when this war is over I shall be able to

---

[36] John was formally promoted to B.S.M. on 11 July, with effect from 3 June.
[37] Passive Air Defense.

prove the extent of my adorations when we have our own little home. I have been dreaming about it a lot since my return.

The journey back was very uneventful. Colin was not exactly over communicative, so I had plenty of time to cast my mind back over the lovely leave. It was all so lovely and heavenly.

It was impossible to force an entry to the buffet car, apart from which it was too hot to shove along the corridor so I remained static and had a pint when I arrived at Bristol and some food when I got up here. It all seems very strange to come back to earth again, and I must confess I miss you terribly. My bed seems so lonely at night without my dear wife, and my day so lonely without her company. Oh that this war would end and we may be allowed to return to each other again.

It was so sweet of you to give me that identification bracelet. I think of you so much each time I see it, which is so often. It has been much admired. George Bishop wants to know the shop it came from. Can you remember?

Well dear heart, no more tonight, must get a little shut eye. God bless you darling heart, and please take care of your precious self for me.

All your adoring husband's love,

Ever yours, Johnnie.

(Horfield Barracks, Bristol)[38] **6 August 1941**

My dearest darling,

I am absolutely at a loss to tell you how upset I am at not writing you more often these days. As I told you, I was down to take a course. This actually started yesterday, so it meant that I had to get things a little shipshape before I left. I feel awfully guilty about it dearest, because I took Sunday afternoon off, and the Quarter and I

---

[38] No address is shown on the letter, this having been added later by John in pencil. John's letter of 7 August provides a possible explanation.

went down to Cheddar. We had intended to get back early, but as we missed the bus, we had to make our own way back as best we could. It was a glorious afternoon. I did so wish you could have been there too. We went via Axebridge. Don't remember you telling me about it? Terribly sweet place. The surrounding place is all you told me it was. I thought of you so much when we went inside the caves, and I was awfully impressed with the glorious colours. We must spend a holiday there some time.

The course here is at first sight very interesting. It's rather amusing to see 70 odd B.S.M.s on parade. At the moment I'm sitting on my bed just before going on parade again. It's one of those double tier bunks. Very precarious to sleep in, and I kept waking last night thinking I was going to fall off. Someone did actually fall off apparently.

There are some amusing blokes here. Will tell you more in my next, but must get this off before parade. Food is wonderful.

Well dearest, no more now. Another letter follows with news.

All my fondest adorations,

Ever most adoringly,

Johnnie.

(Horfield Barracks, Bristol) **7 August 1941**

Dearest Angel,

Thank you so much for a very sweet letter today dearest. It came through from H.Q. Don't worry about the address, they will always forward it.

The lectures here are very security minded, and as far as I can see up until now it's about all there is that I can see in its favour. Remind me sometime to tell you about the lectures on this subject. Too long for a letter! At any rate I've decided to omit the address.

The W.O.s on this course are all (99%) regulars, all having had long service in nearly all branches. I felt so soft giving my service as 3 years, and seeing the name above mine as 23 yrs. Still, I feel it's quite an honour on top of which I'm the youngest by about ten years, and when I tell you how much the course covers in area of troops you'd be quite proud of your Johnnie.

This early morning stint of Reveille at about 06.15hrs doesn't meet with the approval of Johnnie's constitution. I do so miss my tea in bed! The top bunk is very strange, and it does wobble so! Grub is still good – and there's a good helping each time. We shall have a clear day on Sunday, so shall spend a good deal of it in bed. It's a shame I shall not have enough time to get home. By the time we're finished here each night at 7 o'clock, I feel ready for bed. Usually take a walk down the road to get a little fresh air.

Darling, don't know quite what to do about your birthday present. I shall have no time to catch the shops open, so 'fraid it may be a little late darling.

Well my sweetest angel, no more tonight, except my love, and look after yourself.

Ever adoringly,

Johnnie.

(Horfield Barracks, Bristol) **9 August 1941**

Peggy darling,

I received another sweet letter from you today, for which many thanks dear. It's very refreshing to have a few cheerful and refreshing words, and it was a lovely long letter too. You are a darling.

It has been yet another energetic day again though a whole lot more interesting than usual. At last the powers that be have been influenced by requests of the students and are giving us much more valuable instruction on such things as charge procedures etc., and on Monday they are cutting out the marching drill and rifle drill, all of which I think we can safely say we are well up in. Frankly apart from this military law I am very disappointed, and that goes for all people. Still we shall be returning to our units on Tuesday, and I shall not be sorry. There is just one other point that this course has brought home to me, and that is the question of security. I'm going to have a terrific drive when I get back. I'm going to instil into <u>everyone</u> "suspicious alertness" from one or two points I've had brought out in these lectures to me. Peggy, it really is of the utmost necessity. I'll give you a lecture on it next time I see you, and I'm sure you'll realise how even the smallest little item can be used.

It's pouring at the moment. Think I'll go down to the Regiment tonight. It's a curse I can't get back home. Still, the 48hrs won't be long I hope. There will at least be a nice long lie in bed tomorrow, so I'm going to make the best of it. So wish I could be with you darling heart, I do love you so.

All my love darling,

Ever your own,

Johnnie.

(Horfield Barracks, Bristol) **Sunday 10 August 1941**

Darling,

It's a glorious lazy morning here today, with the clocks being put back[39] an hour last night it made a grand night's sleep with the extra late reveille. I must say I feel a whole lot refreshed today.

Have just finished my cleaning etc. and so am taking this opportunity of writing my darling. How are you my dearest heart? I do seem to dream about you a lot these days. It will be heavenly to see you again.

I went down to regimental H.Q. last night. Saw old Geoff Craven. He's attached to R.H.Q. at the moment. Had a very pleasant time with him. We had a good chin wag and a drink. It's quite a long way from here to R.H.Q. so I left, or intended to leave about 9.30, but forgot about the time, which was a bad show, and meant I could only catch a bus to the

---

[39] British Double Summer Time (BDST) lasted from 4 May - 10 August 1941.

63

Centre. It was simply pouring with rain, so I thought I'd go and have some fish and chips, what I done! I met one of the other blokes in there too. Funnily enough he was an instructor at Arborfield while we were there, so we had quite a lot to talk about. Then came the coming back. It's a good hour's walk back to here, and it was absolutely raining heaven's hard. Fortunately I managed to catch a taxi driver who was returning home up this way. He'd refused about fifty people, but I managed to induce him to bring me back, which was a really heaven sent blessing.

I did not tell you yesterday that during a lecture on gas the lecturer had a capsule of D.M.[40] and was showing us how to use it in tests. After explaining what uncomfortable effects it has and the necessity of retaining the respirator in the 'alert' position, he proceeded to light the burner under the salts. There was only the slightest suspicion of the stuff, and it was quite a weak concentration, but the effects were quite terrific. Everyone coughing and spluttering, so much so that the lecture had to be postponed. Believe me, it makes one feel terribly rotten, and I can imagine what a terrible inducement it must be to remove the face piece after having been in a concentration.

Only one more day of this course, thank heaven. It's been rather amusing because most of the instructors are Sgts. As a result they started off on the first day or two being heavy handed. Consequently the blokes on the course decided they'd wear them down, and now instead of the instructors taking us, we take the instructors. Just imagine sixty odd B.S.M.s in a class, nearly all regulars. Their knowledge is pretty good. As a result absolutely nothing gets by unnoticed, and the instructors have learned more than we have.

Well darling, no more news today. I love you terribly, so please look after you,

Johnnie.

---

[40] Dimono-chloro-benzene, a sickness inducing gas.

103 Wharncliffe Gardens, 13 August 1941

Darling,

All the very happiest returns of the day. I don't know when you will get this letter. I feel terribly upset about it sweetheart, it's the first chance I've had of writing to you since Sunday. Monday evening was terribly busy, and there have been so many jobs to do, as well as packing up and coming back from the course. I did not get back much before midday. There were stacks of work to do when I got back, on top of which I had to do a layout of kit. It was not much before 01.00hrs that I turned in last night or this morning. Today we have honestly not had a single spare minute. Several times I started writing, but each time I've been interrupted. Apparently the Colonel[41] is coming here tomorrow on an inspection, and so George is in a bit of a flap and we have to get everything straightened out. So I'm afraid this will arrive rather late to wish you my very sincerest happy returns of the day.

It's 22.30 at the moment, and I've just managed to get off for a few moments to scribble a few lines. I'll have to go back now for a bit more work. George has stacks more to do tonight, will finish writing when we finish.

23.30hrs. Wonders will never cease. Apparently while I was here (my bedroom) writing to you Old George came back from his supper, and after a while he apparently shouted for the Sgt Major. Sgt Roberts said he thought I'd gone to bed. Old George thought it was a good idea, and said he was going to bed. The work apparently can wait till the morning now, so I know what's coming then. It will be a day tomorrow, I can feel it in my bones. What with Colonels and George and his work! Incidentally, you may wonder why all this flap over a Colonel coming round. He has only just taken over command of the regiment, and oddly enough Old George seems to want to impress him. I can't think why. The Colonel is a T.A. man too, and I've told you how George is all for the Regulars. He's a funny cove, and as nice

---

[41] Colonel T. Smith, who took command of 76th H.A.A. Regt on 6 August 1941.

as pie today. He's been consulting me a lot today. Makes me feel really proud to think I'm permitted to have a say in matters and to be able to put in a word or two about the running of the Battery.

It's grand to be back here again, and to have a decent bed to sleep in. Although the course was quite amusing, I cannot say I'm sorry not to have to get up at 06.00hrs, although I woke up at about that time today and could not get back to sleep again. It was rather a sweat on the course, and I must say I'd rather have a hard job here than there.

There were some very pleasant chaps there, and I have been very lucky really, I suppose, to have had the opportunity of going on such a unique course. But that bed on the top bunk was teaser. It used to be quite a manoeuvre to get onto the top shelf.

My little man seems to be very pleased to see me back. I came in and dumped my kit in the room and went straight to work. I had occasion to come back here about an hour later to find he had unpacked for me, and put everything in its usual place, even your photo, which had, as usual, been with me on the course. He's a little gem really. My spare battle dress suit was rather creased in travelling so I find he has pressed and cleaned it for me. It's very pleasant to come back to bed at night and find bread and marge and Bovril waiting for me. Tell Mother I still have it, and have been mean enough to keep it all to me. It's a godsend to have it at night, although I feel I shall need it more in the cold weather.

The weather these last few days has been absolutely appalling, and today it's been more like November than August. Hope it doesn't mean a bad winter to follow. Still, the summer we've had was very pleasant – both days.

Have had one or two "sort outs" with the officers since I've been back and happened to mention it to George in the course of conversation. He seemed quite amused and pleased, and told me to do what I like with them. He doesn't seem to be too fond of them.

Whether this letter comes late or not my darling, it will not prevent my thoughts being with you and wishing you very many happy returns of the day and many more to come, and remember that this letter brings with it my love and adorations.

Ever your own, Johnnie.

103 Wharnecliffe Gardens, Sunday 17 August 1941

Darling,

After the thrill of speaking to you on the phone last night I returned to camp. I can't remember if I told you that the 15th was the first anniversary of army life for about 90% of the Battery. Last night was set aside for one of celebration. Why I can't think, any excuse is better than none I suppose.

By the time I got back beer was practically exhausted. In spite of my intentions to retire for the night I was roped into giving a hand. I had to oblige and sing a song. I hardly need add that it was not exactly refined, but was quite well received. There were numerous turns, good, bad, and indifferent. The general tenor of the affair was quite intoxicated when I arrived and the air was heavy with wafts of alcohol and gruff voices striving to make music while the piano at the other end of the canteen swayed under pints of 'wallop' and heavy thumping on the ivories. Just then the barrel that had been set aside solely for free distribution was opened. So your husband took up his place of honour at the tap filling up the glasses (sneaking a quiet sip here and there) that kept me very occupied until Old George put in an appearance. He had a drink, then I had to quieten the rabble for him to say a few words. It was an exceptionally good speech for George, and, underneath, full of praise for the men. I was one of the few who appreciated what it all meant.

I was not exactly sorry when the bar closed, and what a job ensued getting those blokes out of the place. Worse still getting 'em into bed. I did not feel exactly 'tops' and consequently was not quite so sweet as I might have been. In spite of my resolution it was quite late when I crawled between my blankets.

I have about the greatest honour I could ever have dreamed of bestowed upon me last night. I'll tell you about it. The Gunnery Instructor rang me up yesterday evening. He told me that there is a course being held on Monday, Tuesday, Thursday and Friday for the junior subalterns of the Regiment. Apparently he is unable to take the gun drill so the Colonel has detailed me to take it!!!!!! Me, the junior W.O. of the Regt. I can only think it's an outcome of the inspection he

67

made yesterday. He was really terribly impressed and what I did like was that he didn't try to conceal it. He said that the drill was perfect, and he'd rarely seen Nos 1 who knew their job so well. At any rate never seen the whole lot know so much and be so efficient. I went round like a second class "stooge" on all the inspections. It was a good show, although I say it. At any rate the Sgt Major of the Bty has been selected to train the officers. I feel terribly proud to think that with the very few year's service, and my junior position, I should have been chosen. Rather a good pat on the back for the T.A.

I got up this morning and felt very groggy. So came back to my room when I saw there was nothing important in the office, and lay down on my bed. George came over to see me shortly after and ordered me to bed. I've had a very lazy day, and have slept quite a bit.

Well darling heart, no more tonight, I have quite a lot of reading up to do before the drill tomorrow, I can only hope this headache has gone. I've had it for the last three days.

I hope you enjoyed the dance last night dear heart, do so wish I'd been there too.

All my fondest love and adoration,

Ever most adoringly,

Johnnie.

103 Wharnecliffe Gardens, Tuesday 19 August 1941

Darling,

I had the most wonderful letter from you yesterday morning. You really are an angel and I do so appreciate it. I did love every word of your letter dear heart. Thank you.

Feel a little better this morning. Went to bed very early again last night, so left your letter till this morning. Unfortunately it does not give a lot of time to catch the post. I am writing this in bed, and will have to get up soon. My little man is on 48hrs leave, so will have to induce Jackie to get the shaving water etc.

Had quite an enjoyable afternoon with the officers of the Regt yesterday. The Colonel came up to me and thanked me very much, and said it was an exceptionally good effort. It was only explanatory yesterday. This afternoon I shall have them hopping about a bit. The Colonel watches all the time, and was really pleased yesterday, so this may be another step in the upwards direction for me. He apparently told his Sgt Major he was very impressed with me – See! What a kid!

After I'd finished the drill I came back and did one or two little jobs, and about half an hour in the garden, a little supper, and so to bed. Had a grand night's sleep. So, for now dear, all my love and kisses,

Ever your own,

Johnnie.

103 Wharnecliffe Gardens, 22 August 1941

Darling Sweetheart,

Thank you for your letter today darling. I had to do M.C. of the fortnightly dance here last night, so had no time to write to you dear. I seem to have had every minute crammed since I came back from the course, what with instructions of officers and being in bed. I have no definite news about leave, but hope to be able to let you know tomorrow.

Work is up to knee deep again. Yesterday morning, after I'd had my breakfast, seen the mail, inspected B.H.Q., I decided it was time I had a lesson on the m'bike, what I done! That must have been about 09.45hrs. By 12.00hrs I was out on my own and riding around the village, able to change etc. I feel very proud of myself. I'm not "swinging it" at all, but they will not believe it's the first time I've ever ridden a bike. I have only to be tested, and get a license (all at army expense).

In the afternoon I had my usual class to take. They were better than yesterday, and the Colonel was quite pleased with them. When I got back from the other site, where we have the course, there was a lot to be done, and had to get over to this dance as well.

The dance was very good, considering. Not too many. I only had about two dances. I do so wish I could meet someone of the female sex that I could find a soft spot for and could enjoy talking to and dancing with. You have set such a high standard for anyone else to reach darling. Some of them are quite charming, and I have fixed up with one of them to arrange dancing lessons for the lads. Don't know if it will develop. My "Merry Widow" was there last night. She became quite vampish, and tried to excite your husband's animal instincts, but I soon managed to shelve her.

Have been occupied today mostly on charges. Very odd really that we get one day very good, and then one day umpteen cases, and I have to be the awful Sgt Major and "wheel them in". All stupid charges, and things that could have been avoided, such as improperly dressed on evening leave, absent without leave etc. Takes time.

I had a refresher on the bike again today just so that I don't forget. I seem to be getting on quite nicely, and no longer start off with a huge bounding leap.

Had a wonderful supper tonight, mushrooms, bacon, fried bread, and fried potatoes. It was heavenly, with a pint of beer, and a piece of new bread.

Fondest adorations.
Ever your loving husband,

Johnnie.

103 Wharncliffe Gardens, 25 August 1941

Good morning dearest. How are you today? I'm so sorry I have not been able to write during the last two days. Saturday was quite an occupied day, during which it rained the whole day. I never remember so much water falling from the heavens. The day was filled with the usual little odds and ends with little interest. In the evening

George started on his "standing orders" (for such things as P.A.D. Party, Fire Party, Guard, etc.) which he should have done ages ago, and which I have kept asking him to get cracking on. Saturday evening at about 21.00hrs saw the beginning of the aforesaid. Sunday morning at 02.30 saw the completion of as much as he intended to do. I must admit I was terribly tired yesterday.

Yesterday morning I had to be up early as we had 50 tons of coal coming in, and I had to arrange a platform to put it on. They always choose such ridiculous time to do work in the army. It was a very busy day today too, rushing here and rushing there, and last night George decided to go through his promotions at midnight! He's getting worse. If only he would settle down and get cracking during the daytime all would be well. He potters about by day, and works by night. I curse it because I have not had an evening off since I came back from my course.

Have dreamed of you so much lately. I suppose it was as a result of my hopes for this weekend. I think it will be O.K. I asked George and he said he thought it would, so am praying hard. If you come down darling, I'll meet you at the station if you let me know what time you're coming. Incidentally, if you produce your allowance book it's as good as a pass for reduced fare. Must rush now

All my love dear heart. Am longing for the weekend.

Ever yours adoringly,

Johnnie.

---

7 December 1941
Japan attacks Pearl Harbour.

8 December 1941
USA declares war on Japan.

11 December 1941
USA declares war on Germany and Italy.

Ever your own, Johnnie, Britain, 1938-42

Weymouth, *(undated)* **December 1941**

Subject:- Correspondence, Husband/Wife   Ref. I/LUV/U

To:- The Lady i/c Loveliness,

    Yesterday developed into such an uninteresting day without a cheering letter from my adorable wife. I spent most of yesterday going round the sites with The Great Man. We did not return until about 17.00hrs, I suppose, and that meant it was teatime, so there was no work to be done before the meal. I seem to have been invaded by a very strange feeling at weekends lately, and can summon up no sign of enthusiasm for work at all. I usually start feeling like this on Saturday afternoons, and find it continues until Monday mornings. Today I have felt most lethargic, and had it not been for the fact that The Great Man had gone up to London today, I feel that the picture would have been very different, and that the afternoon would have been spent with the back down. As it was, his absence from the scene of action has given every opportunity to get one or two little jobs done that were rather outstanding. So, with this Saturday afternoon feeling invading my being I tarried long over my tea, chatting with comrades over this and that, and finishing up with a gentle game of patience. When I came back to the office – which was done more out of good spirit than anything else – I found the Great Man pounding up and down the floor, tearing the sole remaining particles of hair from his scalp, and screaming in a very delirious way through a beard of foam, "Find the Sgt Major." People were streaking in all directions, and the whole place looked more like a typhoon than an office. Apparently the trouble had arisen because some dear old fellah had stirred himself into a sitting position whilst performing the duties of fire watcher, and was rather under the impression that our blackout was not complying with the regulations. He then resumed his repose again and troubled us no more, but neither did the Great Man know from whence came the gypsies' warning. So in the normal military manner, the Sgt Major was despatched to locate the cause of the old sage's nightmare. He experienced quite an amount of difficulty, as the night was very wild, and there was a suspicion of mist in the air, and he returned at the end of his journey quite moist. However, the offending light was at last located in the attic of a house way down the road, which has nothing to do with us at all.

Ever your own, Johnnie, Britain, 1938-42

Prior to leaving, the Great Man had told me that I was to take the man's name, and tell him all sorts of frightening stories about having told the police, and how he'd get into trouble etc. When I eventually managed to fight my way through the undergrowth which barred my way to the front door, I found the house was full of Captains, and one or two Majors, to say nothing of lashings of Lts, and I was supposed to stand there and give my party piece in front of this wonderful audience. Because I found that the blackout of the house was as complete as was our own and because I did not give the said officers the Golden Order of the Imperial Rocket, I was to blame for everything. Actually, I thought I did my little piece very well indeed, while the opinion of the Great Man was very different, apparently.

Eventually having managed to pour oil on troubled waters I decided that it would be a very good idea for me to take myself out for the space of an hour or two, and in company with one or two of the lads I went down to the local, where we indulged in a stoup or two of old and mild. It was nearly closing time when we arrived so we did not have much time to get cracking. After they had thrown us out we made our way to the fish and chip shop, and had a portion of fish and chips each. The three ladies at the shop seemed very affable and pleased to see us, as we have not been there for quite a while now. It's been quite a quiet sort of life for the last week or two. Everyone is doing his best to save as much as he can to buy presents. My own modest pocket seems to have acquired quite a bulge. I have as yet been unsuccessful in finding anything in the line I want for you. I may be lucky and find a shop eventually, failing which I shall either send you the money or wait until I come home on my seven days. Incidentally, if I fix my leave for 48hrs at the end of January sometime, and my seven days at the end of February, can you give me some dates for me to work on darling?

I seem to have had a relapse in getting out of bed drill. For a while I was quite a good boy and found it fairly easy to get up early, but for the last week I seem have been a naughty boy. Had a grand breakfast today. For the first time in ages we had eggs. They scrambled them and we had sausages with them. Most tasty!

It was with a very light heart that I was able to say good-bye and good luck to the Great Man, and can honestly say that I have never in all my life before wished that a man is successful on an interview than I felt when I saw the car fade from sight round the bend in the road. Dear

Great I Am, I do hope that he is in luck when he goes before the board!

It has been peaceful here since we bade our fond farewells, the only sound that has broken the silence has been the howling of the wind and the slashing rain against the window panes. Compared with the afternoons when the Great Man is here it has been really quiet. And as he will not be here for three or four days, I'll be able to ring Ruth up. I'm afraid it will be almost impossible for me to get home for the great day[42] unless I can find someone to take me up in a car. At the moment the orders from Army Council state that there shall only be a certain percentage of travel by train. I can assure you that all the vacancies have already been used up, and it would only be possible for me to travel by train at the expense of one of the others, and quite honestly I do not intend to do this. I have a rather slender hope at the moment that it will be possible for me to fix up with the Captain's sister-in-law, as I understand she is going to town and coming back about this time. She is in the W.R.N.S. and has to be back for Christmas Day, as she is on duty, so I am hoping at the moment.

I think that by now I have wasted enough of your time and this paper, so for tonight my darling sweetheart, this is your own little ole man saying goodnight and sweet dreams dearest heart. Remember I love you with all my heart,

Your very own,

Johnnie.

---

[42] The forthcoming wedding of John's sister Ruth to Bob Hall

Wedding of Ruth Kemp and Bob Hall, 23 December 1941.

From left to right: Arthur Kemp, Mrs Hall, John Kemp (as Best Man), Bob & Ruth Hall, Beryl Merrileas (as Maid of Honour), Marjorie Kemp, Robert Hall. Note that John is wearing shoes instead of boots, this being due to him having walked from Weymouth to Poole, some 30 miles, in new boots to catch a bus because of an embargo on train travel, and was as a result suffering from blisters.

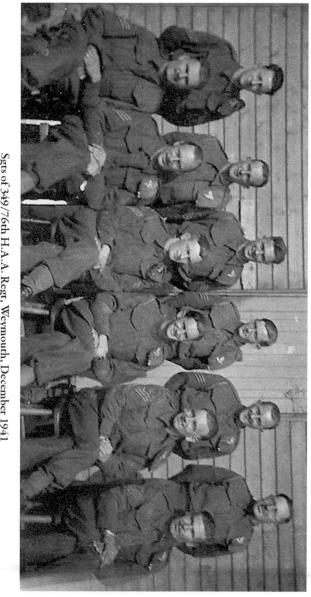

Sgts of 349/76th H.A.A. Regt, Weymouth, December 1941

Back row, left to right: "Robbie" Roberts, Reg Hilton, "B" Bridges, Bob Margetson, Ken Moore, Vic Mogford

Front row, left to right: Ken Mulcaster, Johnnie Johnston, Jackie "Taff" Evans, B.S.M. John Kemp, Jack Shepherd, George Bishop.

1942

Weymouth, 11 January 1942

Dearest Darling,

I have had some quite pleasant news since my return. It appears from what Wag[43] says that George will not be with us very long, which means that Wag will have the opportunity of stepping into his shoes, which will fit him very well. I think he'll make a really wonderful go of it. He's simply bubbling over with keenness and enthusiasm. It is really invigorating to see him. He gives me the feeling of a refreshing spring breeze.

The journey down last night was pretty drear with the most appalling draughts I ever remember. Nearly cut my feet off. Fortunately the compartment practically emptied itself at Basingstoke, and I was able to put my feet up on the seat, which helped alleviate the draught. The train arrived about 23.30hrs, half an hour or so late, and I thought it was colder in Croydon than down here. My doubts were soon put right. I cannot imagine a brass monkey living for a few minutes at last night's temperature. I can assure that my collar was up and my hands deep in my pockets when I walked along the front to get back.

I lay in bed thinking about you so much last night, and sleep was punctured all the way through with visions of you dearest. Winterbourne's apologetic efforts to drag me from bed were not

---

[43] Captain J.J.Wagstaff.

received at all kindly, and the results were very fruitless, and I did not venture a foot out of bed until he told me, in a very troubled state, that it was nearly nine o'clock. All in spite of the fact that I was well nigh "bursting" I clung onto those sheets until it was too much for me.

Today's efforts have been to clearing up the work that always accumulates in so short a time. Can't think where from. It has been a rather unenthusiastic me in the office, and an over enthusiastic Waggie in the other. Full of bright ideas and helpful suggestions about the quickest way to get this or that done, which I'm afraid got no foothold with me. I might play tomorrow, but my thoughts were miles away in Croydon today.

The mess was very empty and quiet. Only Jackie, Robbie, and I, the other three being on leave or on a course. This afternoon was helped considerably by a wonderful patch of sun which spent its whole time moving across the office until it finally disappeared behind the hills. Most pleasing and invigorating. The evening has passed uneventfully and quickly, until I at last find time to write to the dearest darling in the world. It's now midnight, and I think time all Sgt Majors should make tracks for bed.

All my fondest love, adorations and kisses. Good night and God bless you.

Ever your own,

Johnnie.

Weymouth, 2 February 1942

My Own Dearest darling Sweetheart,

How can I begin to tell you how very heavenly it was to have been with you for this last week. It does seem so strange to be writing to you again and not being able to tell you in person. I do miss you so darling. I have been thinking about you all day, and wondering just where you were.

Hope you managed to settle up alright. I feel very disappointed that the "billet" was so very miserable, and I suppose you had the inevitable sausages for breakfast. I have made a vow that as long as I'm in Weymouth I shall not go there again.

I hope that the journey was alright dearest, and that you did have lunch and managed to get a porter at Waterloo and Croydon. That case was far too heavy for you to carry.

I managed to get back without detection from higher quarters. It was lucky I left when I did as George[44] was in the office quite early. It's been dreadful today. Apart from the first effects of being back to earth again, George has been just like a raving lunatic all day. He eventually went upstairs at about 21.45, after which I met Tom Dale in the canteen and had a drink, and here I am to write to my wife. Shall retire soon, as I have to be up since 05.45hrs to go on this wretched trip out in the country. We have to leave here at 07.30hrs on Wednesday for this course. I have the feeling it will be a fiasco, but we'll see.

I do so miss your sweet company so very much. The day has seemed so lonely, and bed so very uninviting. Suppose I've got to get used to it again. Must go to bed now dear.

All my fondest adorations, and sincerest thanks, ever most adoringly,

Your very own husband,

Johnnie.

Weymouth, 14 February 1942

My own Darling Valentine,

What will you be thinking of me for not remembering earlier, I just cannot dare to think. It was the first thing I thought of when I

---

[44] "George" was promoted from 349 Battery to become 2 i/c 76th H.A.A. Regt on 3 February 1942, subsequently transferring to 110th L.A.A. Regt in May 1942. Cpt Wagstaff became O.C. of 349 Battery on 3 February 1942.

woke this morning. After I went up to the office I regret to say that the thought was completely pushed out of my mind by a hundred and one little things, and it wasn't until I received that sweet and lovely card that I remembered again. I kept thinking all day that there was something I'd forgotten, and couldn't think what it was. I'm livid to think I did not remember before. Dates have all seemed so messed up this last week. I have been signing letters as March since I've been back from the course. I ask no forgiveness and feel none is due. I never remember feeling such a dreadful tyke. All I can say is, dear heart, my love for you on this Valentine's day is greater and sweeter than ever before. It's too late to do anything about it all, and I must just vow it will never happen again.

Thank you so much for the card darling. I did think it was a wonderful effort, and I did love it. I also had your sweet and welcome letter dearest. I have been so depressed today. Can't think why. Everything here is going so well too. Your letter was the brightest spot of the day and cheered me up quite a bit. I think all this news lately is really most annoying, and I just can't help wondering what we're going to do about it. It will come soon I know, but I do wish we'd started earlier.

You rather seem to be worrying too much about the long pants business dear. I can assure you that I don't really need them. Admittedly it has been cold, but I never wore "pants woollen, long" before I started my military career and I see no reason why I should continue to do so. I don't really miss them, else I should have worn them before. Also rest that little head on the question of the Halibut Oil. I finished the original bottle on the prescribed date, having not missed a single dose and am now on the second dose. I honestly think that they are wonderful medicine. I know I feel 100% better for taking them. I'm so glad you put me onto them again.

The transformation of the coat looks and sounds most interesting and attractive Peg. I had completely forgotten about that coat, and always loved it. It does bring back a host of memories.......

There has been an interval of about an hour since I wrote the above. Winterbourne came in about that time. But I should start at the beginning. He was due back from 48hrs leave last night at 23.59hrs. When I found this morning that he had not returned I was terribly upset. I knew he was not the sort of bloke to "mike", and felt sure something must be wrong. I held up the Absentee Report I should have sent to R.H.Q. by the first D.R.[45] this morning until lunch time hoping some news might come through, but as I'd heard nothing I had to send it in. He's just arrived now. Apparently he's been having trouble with his mother. She's an invalid and I gather slightly simple. The poor lad seems rather beside himself with worry. Fortunately he did do the right thing and applied to the nearest unit for an extension, which was granted. It was then their duty to inform us of what they had done. The whole family seems odd. Father has been away from home for years, and there's a brother who's fond of the bottle, and a married sister who doesn't seem to do much to help. Winty is the only one who does anything. I feel very sorry for him.

I must inform you that under the Waggie regime I do NOT, repeat NOT work late. Waggie loves his bed as much as I do, and loves early nights even more. He's very rarely at work after 22.00hrs at night. Office work, as far as outside influences are concerned has subsided considerably. There is a whole heap of work to be done, but fortunately this can be done at a more reasonable time. I'm rather late tonight owing to the fact that Wag and I are working out a scheme for the second course (similar to the one I was on)[46]. It will be starting at 19.30 tomorrow, and goes on till 22.00hrs. We've both got to go as critics. I have to go on the M/C. Should be great fun. Wag and I are going to the other side of Dorchester tomorrow morning, and he's asked if I know of any good hotels in the district, so it may mean lunch as well.

The work at the training camp[47] next month sounds terrific, and we should emerge 1st class soldiers if we survive the course.

Wag came back from leave today full of the "family". He's terribly thrilled with "it". Calls it "Jane". He brought me some special 'baccy. Thought I might like it. Rather sweet I think, don't you?

---

[45] Dispatch rider.
[46] Simulated attacks on 76th H.A.A. units, together with mobile and communications exercises.
[47] Drake Lines, Blandford Military Camp, Blandford Forum, where anti-aircraft units received mobility training under 11th A.A. Brigade and A.A. Mobile and Tactical Training Centre.

Had a consolidated bill for my phone calls today for December and January. He wouldn't let me pay it until he received an authenticated account. He thought the original one, which was for December, was incorrect. The total now comes to 19/8! So I've had to shake the old pockets about a bit. It does seem a little steep, but one cannot argue with the phone company.

Alex and Jackie have just gone to bed. Before they went Alex asked if I were writing to you, and then asked me to send his regards and hopes you are well. Jackie Evans saw the Valentine card and asked me to tell you that he's wished that you had sent it to him instead of me. He feels he deserves it more than I do (chuckles from Alex, and mutterings of "What's the matter with your other ladies?"). The card was greatly admired by the lads.

Robbie went on 48hrs today, so it now leaves the mess rather empty, since Jack Shepherd and Maurice Page are on this course. Don't think Shep's too happy having to sit and listen to George all day long. He does hate "Hookie" as he calls him. I'm so glad George is no longer with the Bty. I feel Jack S would have spoilt his chances of B.S.M. I don't think they're too good as it is.

George Bishop has been asking after you lately, and asks me to remember him to you. The lads seem to have taken a great liking for my wife. Can't blame them. It shows good taste.

Saw Geoff Craven yesterday. In fact had lunch with him at Wyke. He's as miserable as ever, and now has more to worry and grumble over. Poor Kathleen has been sent her calling up papers for the A.T.S.!!! I leave you to imagine how they have been received. I can just picture the two chewing it over. Geoff says he will get her out of it. Don't know how! I must say I thought the wife of a soldier was exempt, feel sure I'm correct.

We have a regimental dance next Friday. Don't know that I want to go, but feel I shall have to. There will be a lot of trouble caused if I back out since I've been sent an invitation (no paying this time!). Wish you were here to go darling, it would be so lovely. Suppose you can't manage the weekend can you?

No more now dearest dear. I must off to my empty bed. Wish you were here.

All my fondest love and kisses dearest,

Ever most adoringly, your very own hubbie,

Johnnie.

Weymouth, 19 February 1942

Peggy Darling,

The postman has once again passed me by, and it seems that for today I'm not going to be lucky with a letter. My dearest heart, I do so hope that there is nothing wrong. I am longing for that home of ours darling, we do seem to have waited so patiently. It just seems unbelievable that it's now getting on for three years that we've been parted like this. It will be three of the most valuable years wasted. I miss you so very much.

I feel so helpless and useless stuck away here. If I could only think I was doing something to help bring this war to an end. Admittedly there is a rather more active role ahead, but I feel it's rather useless. Had it not been for you I would have applied for a transfer to a more active life, but it's not quite fair to transfer to the Navy with a wife who I adore so much.

I can never remember being so busy as I have been today. My head is absolutely spinning. It has just been one thing after another, and there seems no end to it. Just before I came down to supper a mass of work came in and it's all to be done tonight, heaven alone knows how. 'Fraid the early night resolution will break down today. Wish Robbie were here instead of on a course, as it makes the job doubly hard. It's all useless in the majority, and will never be wanted. But that's how it is, and that's how we lose our possessions, and how all the time we're "prepared". It does make me sick.

Things seem to have gone wrong with everyone today. I just seem to have caught people on the wrong foot all day. Have several on charges for their wrong doings too.

83

I am enclosing 10/- towards the bag darling. I also thought that the enclosed cake of soap might be acceptable. I am a week up on my coupons at the moment. We are now issued with one soap coupon per week, and as one of these cakes lasts me a week and a half, I hope to be able to send you more.

I am the only one left in the mess tonight. All the rest except Jackie Evans are on courses. Jackie has taken himself out for the evening. I'm afraid he'll come back the worse for wear as he's gone out with Arthur Franklin.

Waggie was full of beans today, although he is not using polite language about the work that there is to be done. Had a chat about Jane today. I've never seen anyone so proud of his family as he is.

Well my dearest there seems to be little news tonight, and that ------ work is just screaming to be done. Supper has not yet arrived, so will go back and do some more work.

There are 15 more days until 48hrs leave, and am just counting the days and minutes until the 7th.

All my fondest love and kisses darling,
Ever your very own,

Johnnie.

Weymouth, 20 February 1942

Darling,

Thank heavens I received your letter today. It was a wonderful relief. Have had another rushing day. Have been all over the place. Felt much better tonight having heard from my wife. She is so adorable.

Have had another minor offence session today. Hope that will be the last. The general tone of the Bty has gone up 100%. Wag is champion at encouraging enthusiasm, being all enthusiastic himself, it sort of glows everywhere he goes. Had a Brigadier visit scare today. Much rushing round in circles. I was amazed how much more enthusiastic

Geoff has become. He's going to be damn useful if he continues like he is at the moment.

We have the Regimental Dance tonight. I shall toddle down later. Do wish my wife were going to be there. It should be quite a posh affair.

Awfully little news tonight darling heart. Will try to add more in the morning. All my love for tonight dearest, Johnnie.

21st Feb I realised this morning that tomorrow is Sunday, so have held this letter over to write tonight's edition. In last night's letter I left you just before I went to the dance. As a dance it was one gigantic frost, and B.S.M. Kemp was seen tripping the light fantastic on one occasion only. I don't know quite what went wrong, I was willing enough in spirit, and feel sure my feet did well, but neither of us had the slightest control over those boots. One dance and one dance only! At one period during my wrestling match with a very demure young thing my left foot became ensnared with a portion of the stickiest and most unreasonable piece of cake I've yet met (that's one of the drawbacks of refreshments in the dance hall). This might not have proved disastrous had it not been that my right foot suddenly took leave to travel at great speed in the other direction. Fortunately, the demure young thing had a dress designed to save falling S.M.s, and I had just made one wild grab at one or two bits that seemed to have no reason for being there at all. Fortunately - at first - they took the strain and I began to think I should retain my balance, until suddenly someone behind me also became enmeshed with the remainder of said cake, and emulated my antics. I saw it coming from my precarious position. It was too late to avert the crash, so I just steeled myself for the thud. It came. My partner was definitely built for comfort, not manoeuvrability. It rather goes without saying that my retirement from the mêlée was carried out in good order, and I retreated to a previously prepared position from which point of vantage I took a healthy view of festivities from the other end of a glass. My partner had "a promise of a car lift home", my last recollections of the good lady was firstly a great display of petticoats and many coupons worth of "pretties", followed by a very hasty withdrawal from the scene of battle. I rather spoilt things by resorting to that rude guffaw I am wont to at times. And that my dear wife is but one argument in favour of dancing lessons for your lord and master.

Needless to say, although this was my first public appearance in the guise of a Russian ballet dancer, I can assure you my career in that direction is now over.

Having taken my body to the bar, I managed to find a break in the defence which had gathered there, and pushed my carcass into a position of vantage from where I could command attention, and a fair portion of the bar to sprawl across. I then proceeded to pour alcoholic stimulant down into my 'stomick'. The remainder of the boys put in an appearance, and we went the rounds. I should be ashamed to admit it, but I wondered exactly what had hit me when I woke up this morning. But my behaviour has been good lately, and this was my first whole evening of this week. It was good really, and I enjoyed it, apart from the dance. I was never constructed to be a Fred Astaire. I realised today how dreadfully unpleasant those Halibut oil capsules can be. Not feeling too bright this morning I had – rather naturally in view of what must have been mixed in my 'stomick' - indigestion, and nearly all day I have been eating Halibut.

Incidentally, I discovered today that the wretched Winterbourne had not despatched the shoes, so after brassing him up, I did so today. You should get them about the same time as this letter. Hope you received the soap etc. Let me know if it was all there O.K.

Reference your letter received yesterday, please be assured my darling I am writing home regularly. I've been a very good lad lately in that respect. Hope to be able to spend an afternoon, perhaps tomorrow, writing to all the people I've not written to for ages (which is typical, either he writes and goes bald headed at it, or he does not write at all. What a man!!).

Has been very cold here today, and has snowed quite a bit. Have been occupied trying to sort out a man who "did a bunk" from the guard room nearly all day. If only these people realised how much time and trouble they cost. Perhaps they do. Maybe their reason for so doing.

Had a football match here on a piece of waste ground s'art'noon. It was interrupted by an alarm. First for days. The gun park looked quite colourful with football jerseys and socks showing beneath great coats. I think they must have been raiding shipping in the Channel. The plots spent a while going round in circles until it was reported that Spitfires had gone up to intercept, and they beetled off.

Well dearest, have reached the end of paper and news. It's now only 14 more days until 7th, and so longing to see you dearest. Give my love to Mother and Father, and to yourself dearest all the love in the world.

Ever your very own adoring husband,

Johnnie.

Weymouth, 24 February 1942

My own darling wife,

I was terribly thrilled to receive your letter today. I can never let you know how much it bucked me up.

I have had another day when I've been absolutely so rushed I've not known where I've been rushing to next. Started off this morning with a trip into Regiment at crack of dawn with a lorry load of "accused, evidence, and escort" to be seen by the Colonel. I was disappointed with the results obtained and punishments awarded. The ones who should have received heavy sentences got off very lightly, including one bright youth who broke out of the guard room whilst under close arrest. The ones who should have got off were rather heavily caned I thought. It's a funny army.

There is a grand sort out of junior N.C.O.s at the moment, and those who are no good are losing their tapes. It's time too. George pushed men up on Officer's recommendations who were no good at all. Waggie is more particular, and does listen to my views on the subject.

As I write this every time I look up I see stacks of letters round me marked "BSM" "BSM to see" "BSM please get" etc. Waggie's greatest fault is that everything that comes in he promptly shoots out to me. I went in to see him about 1700hrs today, and said I could not take anymore for today. It's fantastic. I've enough to keep me going for 24hrs solid. I spoke too soon when I said that there was not much doing. It has just come down from Regiment in shoals during the last few days, and I have so much to do out doors, especially with my driving lessons. I don't know if I told you, but I have to be able to drive all the vehicles we possess, and the list is very long.

Well darling, it's now 23.40, and I feel quite sleepy, so will close this letter. Incidentally ref leave, wouldn't it be possible for you to get the night of 7th, or the night of 9th in the view of my 72hrs? Do let me know when to fix it up darling. So very excited at it all.

Fondest love dearest,

Johnnie.

Weymouth, 1 March 1942

My Darling Peggy,

Thank you for your letters darling. I have not had a minute to reply. Thank heaven at last I have been able to get out a bit. For the last four or five days it's been out doors all day, and office work by night. Consequently I have had a lot to do. We have started very seriously on this mobile racket and I have been out everyday and all day since I last wrote you.

I have provisionally arranged for my leave to start on 6th March, as I thought it would be better to have a night without you at the beginning of my leave than at the end. I presume that you will be at home until 16.00hrs on 6th, so shall be able to see you from 13.00hrs until 16.00hrs.

You'll be pleased to know that I became War Substantive W.O.II (B.S.M.) yesterday. So they cannot take it away except by Court Martial now. This also means an extra 2/6 per week for you for the nine months I've held the appointment, and an extra 2/6 per week for each succeeding week of holding the rank. So that's 2/6 a week to the good for the rest of the war I hope.

I have to be up at 05.30 tomorrow dearest, and it's now 23.30, so hope you'll excuse more. I am going on a big scheme tomorrow and that's same for rest of the week. I don't know when will finish. Will try to write more tomorrow.

In great haste,
All my adorations darling,

Johnnie.

Weymouth, 15 March 1942

My own dearest darling,

Many thanks for your letter dated 11 Mar. It was very sweet and dear of you to write when I know you are so busy.

Since I wrote to you last I have been desperately busy with more late nights. The work has poured in left right and centre. It's all been rush work, and had to be done. We certainly are doing well in our effort of using paper in this army, a little less of which would go a long way to helping the way I feel. I've also been clearing up of the charges laid against prisoners of the early part of the week. To do punishment in the army is a most destroying experience. Three I have here now work from 06.00hrs to 19.00hrs with only ½ hour break for meals, no smoking etc. I think it's wise to "keep clean".

I had to be a witness in producing evidence against a man, who is going up for Court Martial, all day yesterday. Meant a lot of work. He was absent for 52 days!! And they think they are being hard done by.

Saw Jackie Shepherd yesterday, looked very fit, and asked after you. Alex is away sick on leave at the moment. Think he's rather groggy by the sounds of things. Robby is on leave and so am finding the going rather heavy at the moment.

I did ½ an hour's shooting with Waggie yesterday. He's got a grand little .22, and it's deadly accurate. Waggie has today become Major Wagstaff!!

Am dreadfully rushed for time dear. The delay in this letter has been unavoidable dear. I do so hope you'll understand. There may be even more delay later this week and next. Look after yourself dearest heart.

Ever adoringly, your very own,

Johnnie.

Weymouth, 18 March 1942

My Darling,

Thank you for your wonderful letter today. I did so appreciate it dear, especially as I felt soaked to the skin and thoroughly dejected. We had a night exercise yesterday starting about 14.00hrs eventually arriving back here at 10.45hrs today. The route stretched quite a good distance away[48]. I started off later than the rest as I had a lot of work to do. I had hoped I might be excused, but I was detailed to go, already having evaded the first scheme. The weather was quite pleasant when I left here, but by the time I got into hilly country the visibility was down to about 50yds owing to a very low cloud ceiling. There were occasional spasms where I came down to villages where the sun was shining. I eventually located the main party about 17.00hrs, and after an apology for tea, and an outsize sandwich we "upped sticks" and moved again. By the time we reached our destination it was pitch dark.

The only sleeping accommodation was in one of five lorries, which were needed for the men. Geoff Craven scouted round and found a haystack, which he recommended very strongly as being dry and warm (it had been raining most of the evening incidentally). So Geoff, I and another Sgt made our way through a sea of mud with our bedding, and after much manipulation, we wedged ourselves into the side of the haystack. It all seemed quite homely at the time, but we did not know what was to come. We all felt tired, and sleep was not difficult. I awoke at 01.30hrs to find Geoff's left boot in the middle of my face. After politely enquiring what it was doing there, I was informed that its owner was trying to find if there was a gap in the barbed wire

---

[48] Sussex and Hampshire.

surrounding the haystack. Further inquiry, enlightened by the use of a lamp electric, showed that a massive bull had its head wedged in the wire fence. I was most impressed by the huge ring it had through its nose, and the clouds of steam emitting from its nostrils. It couldn't have been more than three feet from me, and I could feel the warmth of its breath. Geoff was running round in ever decreasing circles trying to "shoo" it away. The bull was standing there with its head stuck, pawing the ground. It managed to extricate itself eventually, and Geoff made a rapid exit to the safe side of the haystack. I had a vision of an onslaught from the beast, but he just trotted away, having found a sweet young cow. I breathed a sigh of relief and after Geoff's disturbing efforts to bed down again, was just dozing off when two strange crawling insects – which I imagined as huge hairy spiders – infiltrated into the blankets. After a running fight, I retired to a fortified position on the other side of the bed, and left their occupied area to the invaders. They were apparently satisfied for I was not troubled by them anymore.

My next efforts at sleep were rudely interrupted by a complete change of wind (atmospheric pure and simple!) from behind the haystack to our front. It brought with it torrential rain. So in exasperation I just pulled the ground sheet over my head and hoped for the best. I came away today with half the haystack down my back, and the other half in my hair.

It poured all the way home, and I could feel water between my toes, so I promised I'd have a bath when I got back. It was just as I was about to have a bath when I received your dear letter. It did cheer up my dampened spirits considerably.

Well darling, it's 23.59hrs exactly, so will get some shut-eye. Night night darling.

All my fondest love dearest,

Your very own husband,

Johnnie.

349/76 H.A.A. Regt R.A.
c/o G.P.O. Havant, Nr Portsmouth, Hants.
Wednesday 8 April 1942

My own Lovely Lady,

Your precious letters have come as medicine to me. It has
meant a lot to me to have these letters dearest. I do so want to thank
you for the gloves you sent me Peggy. How terribly sweet of you
darling. They really are magnificent, you have no idea how much I
value and cherish them. Thank you so very much my dearest. Had
there been time dear I would have written you before. You know that,
but I have wasted so much time apologising in the past, that I'll do my
best to give an account of my self up to now.

When I wrote to you last I cannot remember. Life at Blandford was
really desperate. I never got to bed until after midnight, and reveille
was seldom after 06.00hrs. I have never realised that there is such a
short time between 06.00 and 09.00hrs. During this time there are
always umpteen fatigues to get on parade or guards when you're Duty
Bty. Otherwise there is always a "scheme". I always have to be there
too. It's bad enough getting men off alone, but when there's umpteen
vehicles as well it's a big job.

I had several very pleasant days out. I was allocated a m'bike just
before we left B'ford. A 350 Royal Enfield. I must say I was not very
excited about it, not enough punch and stability.

We came down here quite recently, and the two days before we left we
were doing "schemes" right up to the "off". The journey down was
quite enjoyable. I came down on above mentioned M/C. I had not
been in the camp more than a couple of hours, and had to make
another journey of about a mile, in the course of which I was about
100yds from my destination when there was an awful knocking noise
from the 'works' under me, and discovered that the bearing on the big
end had gone! I was livid. On inspection we discovered that the oil
supply was faulty. I checked the sump before I left, and it was full.
When we looked after the incident it was empty. I think the journey
was too much for her. Convoy work is very strenuous for a bike that's
run in, and this being a re-bore job really ought not to have been used

for this. I feel upset, as I am careful with these bikes. There are plenty of others who use them carelessly, and I feel as though I've been placed in their category. The real trouble was that I have become used to a dry sump, and not really having to worry about changing under 2,000 miles. With a wet sump, as the Enfield has, I should have continually checked the consumption of oil until I know all its merits etc. Still, I have got the "tiffys"[49] working on it, and hope it will be ready this weekend. It's difficult to get the soft metal bearing, so just have to hope.

Since I've been here I have been almost confined to the office. There has been a ridiculous influx of "bumph" to make matters worse. It has meant that on the few occasions I've been out I have set too at about 21.00hrs, and usually get to sleep about 02.00 – 03.00hrs. I never remember feeling so tired and worn out as at the moment. Unfortunately it's not like it was before where I could pack up and leave things. The ------- stuff has to be done there and then. The only consolation I have, which is not much really, is that everyone else is doing just as much. I shall be thoroughly glad when this is all over. The initial enthusiasm has been rather dampened by the long hours. To make matters worse I can see no way of getting home for the 1st. There is a chance though of 9 days leave about 16th May so Wag says. I'm praying for it. Thank God I have you to think about dearest. This is real commando training, and sorts out those who cannot take it, and there are quite a number.

My angel, this is but brief, and I hope there will be more chances now I'm straighter. I do love you so very much darling, and have had you in my thoughts continuously though I've not written. Well darling heart, my fondest adorations, and please look after my darling wife, I love her so.

Ever your own adoring husband,

Johnnie.

P.S. Ruth wrote me saying Tich now has "wings" and commission, and is on leave in New York prior to coming home.

---

[49] Army nickname for Artificers (skilled motor mechanics).

21 June 1942
Rommel captures Tobruk.

c/o G.P.O. Dover, 5 July 1942

Dearest darling,

From the seclusion of a gloriously peaceful Kentish village to one of the outposts of England. Right up on top of the "White Cliffs"[50] within sight of France. Your pink haired one battles his way from duty to duty in the teeth of a gale. I cannot say it's the back of beyond, it's in front of anything I've seen as far as a position goes. For the remainder we're doomed to stay in our rocky fortress until our next leave. The pathway (I could hardly say roadway) is very steep, perilous, and winding. I have to get into first and put the brakes on when going down. Apart from the wind - I should not like to see it really blow here.

It has been glorious weather until a rather violent thunderstorm last night. The view of France in the evening is very good through binoculars etc. There's one little Fritz we do not like the look of. He's got ginger hair and is cross-eyed. Each morning Robbie wakes and says "He's on sentry duty again," and each one in turn sticks his tongue out to the direction of the enemy.

There was a spectacular searchlight display the other night, and both sides tried to see who could outdo who. Can't imagine what it was for.

The journey down here was quite pleasant. Came through Canterbury. It looks rather sad and sore nowadays. The Cathedral still stands intact as far as I could see. I'm still impressed by the lovely views in this part of the world, although fields and roads are lined with yards and yards of barbed wire and masses of diligent guards. I shall not venture out at

---

[50] Farthingloe battery, gun site D1, the Regiment having moved to Dover 3 July from Gravesend, where they had been posted on 16 May. No letters by John between 8 April and 5 July have, if any, survived.

nights. This is more dangerous since everywhere is heavily mined. Haven't seen much of the Luftwaffe, suspect our suspense will not be long delayed.

Conditions here are much more like the real McCoy, although red tape is still predominant. Just can't get away from it. The usual late nights have been unavoidable since the first mention of move. It was very sudden and unexpected. Hope to get things sorted out soon. There's precious little to go out for here, and it's a deuce of a climb back to the camp.

I'm not impressed by Dover on my visit there on motorcycle, it seemed a scruffy place. The Brig here is a grand little fellow, and very short in stature. They call him "Two Bottles High".

There is so little I can tell you in my letters nowadays, as there is so much more need for it than ever before, as you doubtless appreciate. In case you are worrying about something, I can definitely tell you "<u>NO</u>", not yet anyway. There's been no mention.

I miss you more than ever down here. I still have my fingers crossed for 25th. Thank heavens it's not so far off now. No more now dearest. All my love darling,

Ever adoringly,

Johnnie.

Dover, 10 July 1942

Hello my Cherub,

So very many thanks for the batch of most delightful letters you sent me. I did so enjoy reading them. Do wish I could manage time to write more to you than I do these days. The frantic flap continues. Thank you so much for the flints you sent me. I appreciate the thought immensely, they will be most useful and welcome.

12 July. Today completes a most hectic day or two, and I am really pleased things are cooling down again. I was interrupted in the middle of the above, and have had no time to complete since. I wouldn't mind so much if it were all confined to daytime, but it's been nights as well lately. Here's what happened:

Friday 10 July. Informed the night before there was an inspection by downwards from the Field Marshal! There's a flap if the Colonel inspects. Imagine the flap they had with a rank of this magnitude. The evil brains got together and decided that reveille would be 05.30hrs!! This meant I was up quite a lot earlier.

14 July. Once again I will attempt to write, I am determined to finish this time. We had a series of alarms after I'd written last time, and did not stand down until nearly 3. Nothing much over. 'Fraid it's all been rather difficult this last week. The move always makes more work, on top of which Robbie, Jackie Evans, and Maurice Page have been on leave. Yesterday Jack Shepherd was sent out to a troop. Leaves only Alex and me in the office.

As I was saying when I wrote last. The whole camp had to be cleaned by 09.00hrs. We just managed it by the skin of our teeth. He was quite a decent old stick, although absent minded. Introduced himself to me three times and asked if I'd served in India. Discovering I was T.A., he asked what I had done in civvie street, and appeared most interested in it all. He was of course attended by a galaxy of talent, all smothered in red and gold braid. Most impressive really. "Two Bottles" was there. Looked ridiculous beside Waggie.

The next day was supposed to be an inspection by the Corps Commander. Same reveille and cleaning up. But he did not turn up. Most annoying. I often wonder what impression these inspections give to the people inspecting. It should be most favourable after all the work put in.

Thank you for your letters dearest. They have been most refreshing in this outlandish spot miles from the back of nowhere. Have not yet had an evening off so don't know what happens outside. Did have a break yesterday when I had to contact the local A.P.S.[51] Seemed strange to meet civilians again. What I've seen of Dover in my fleeting dashes through on a motorbike, it seems normal and quite pleasant.

I am counting the days until I see you again. I'm sorry about the 24th instead of 25th. Suppose it can't be helped. Pity. But I quite understand.

Well darling "salvage" conscious wife, must rush. Have heaps to tell you when I get home. Can't mention in letters, especially from here. Hope to write more often as Rob comes back today. I love you dear.

Ever your own,

Johnnie.

Dover, 16 July 1942

My darling,

I had your letter today, thank you. I had every intention of carrying out my promise this afternoon of writing to you, but after lunch I sat in a chair and went to sleep until tea time, consequently I had to make up time this evening. Have felt very sleepy today. It's been very muggy and damp with quite a heavy sea mist.

Life seems to progress in its usual way here. Nothing very different. We seem to be developing into a welfare society at the moment, and nearly all our time seems to be spent in sorting out private affairs of the lads. I feel that perhaps we are a little too soft in some cases. Have been trying to clear up matters of a man who continually receives letters and telegrams from his wife that either she or one of the children is ill. It now appears that she lives with her mother and sister, and should imagine gets "beaten up" by them. So have written to see what can be done tonight.

Waggie has had the day off. Going home to Jane's Christening. Have quite a lot to tell you about him when I come home. I think I might

---

[51] Army Postal Service.

catch the train on the evening of 23rd with a bit of luck. Shall see how it goes. It's only a week from today. It seems ages since I was last home. Hope the weather brightens up somewhat.

Am feeling dreadfully sleepy, so will close now. All my fondest love dearest dear.

Goodnight darling,

Your most affectionate and adoring,

Johnnie.

Dover, 21 July 1942

My dearest darling heart,

Many thanks for all letters to hand. You're a sweetheart to write me such dear letters.

Very hectic time again since I wrote last, culminating in the last 36hrs. Had to post away a large number of "unfits" and take in replacements yesterday. Once again that weird think in the army brain decided they'd catch a train away from here in the middle of "sleeping time", which meant getting up at 04.00hrs. Collecting sleepy – not to mention dopey at the best of times or else they wouldn't have gone – Gnrs at that time of the morning is ghastly. It's bad enough collecting me. Then you discover that someone's missing just as you're about to move off. Apparently no one's seen him. We search everywhere. Zero hour is approaching. Finally find the dopey one back in bed again asleep. I told him his history, and he nearly "went spare". Give him five minutes to be outside with the others. It's pitch dark. I go back to the party and find only two or three left by the aid of a very dim torch. They look dreadful. One trailed over the back of a lorry asleep, one of the other two asleep on their kit bag. The one awake tells me that the others have gone to spend numerous pennies. Give the Bdr i/c a kick where he can't see and tell him he'll be going up before the O.C. Finally, just as it starts to rain, we're ready. Arrive at the station to find we're the first Bty to arrive. Remainder trickle in ½ and ¾ hr later. Officer i/c on last truck has flap as train is due. I salute and melt into distance. It's his pigeon now. Get back to camp and have hot cup of tea and then a marvellous hot shower, clean up, and sort out oddments of int[52]. Two kippers for breakfast, and fresh milk on Shredded Wheat! Office most of day. Then fire drill, and inspection of camp with R.S.M. He thinks conditions very hard and unnecessary. Says he'll see what he can do. Doubt if he'll do much. Dinner is late, so feeling sleepy I get "horizontal". Am woken every few minutes by Sgts, Bdrs, and Gnrs, "Can I have my fags for week." "Will you inspect guard now, sir." "Mrs Prentice[53] has sent Gnr P. telegram, reads 'Edith still very ill'." (There'll be another tomorrow I expect). Eventually batman walks in to tell me it's 15.30hrs, do I want lunch? Curse awful at him. Say why didn't he wake me before. Office all afternoon on accidents reports and correspondence. See a Scot who has trouble with two sons and daughter of a family of ten!!! Daughter only sixteen and "going aroond wi' a Bomadierrrrrrr"!! Fix him up. Goes away very content and grateful. Have tea and game of crib with Robbie. After tea make out a list of more people we don't want, stating reasons. Takes a long time until supper. Bread, paste, and tea. Ugh! See Scot again after tea. Hear more details. Admire him for action he apparently took on last leave. Conference with Waggie, for now more office work. Then beer in canteen with Robbie, Jackie Evans, and Waggie. Back to mess in time to be greeted by message I'm wanted in office. Finish that and I'm down to station to meet new men. Look awful in the dark. Masses of stiff caps and paper parcels. Soon get rid of those. Bring them back to give them supper at 01.30hrs. Then show them billets and draw blankets. All go to bed about 02.30hrs. Very tired.

21 July. Kicked in pants by batman at 09.55hrs and given message from office. Am still in bed. Get frantic. Ask why I haven't been up before. Am told by terrified looking batman I couldn't be woken up. Knock over cold cup of tea beside bed. Cut myself while shaving. Can't get hair to lie down, and find boots have not been cleaned and covered in mud. Am in foul temper at breakfast, I hate being late. Besides, I

[52] Intelligence.
[53] Name changed to protect identity.

have a headache. Feel dreadful. Mouth like disused cesspool. Have been smoking cheap tobacco lately and burned tongue.

After breakfast inspect camp. Much "beating up". Get place straight. Fire drill, and up to gun park with Waggie. Take new recruits to O.C. separately for interview. Some quite bright. Majority ghastly. Have just had lunch, and shall go back to office in a few minutes…….. And that my angel is as much as I can write today as I have a lot to do.

I'm so excited about the leave darling. It will be grand to be with you again. I don't quite know whether I shall be able to manage Thursday or not. I can only phone you to let you know I'm on my way.

Fondest love,

Johnnie.

P.S. Failing Thursday I shall be home Friday at about 08.30hrs.

Dover, 10 August 1942

My own darling sweetheart,

Have been meaning to write for the last few days. Must say how sorry I am not to have been able to do so before.

Life has taken a completely new line lately, once again we go back to the busy days of much rushing and excitement. Robbie went on leave on Friday evening, and comes back today. That's always an excuse for more work for me. I realised last night that I've been back only just over a week. Seems like years. I miss you terribly.

Now, where did I leave off when I last wrote you. I feel so mean letting it go so long. Perhaps the outstanding event was Saturday afternoon last. We had Regimental Sports. I spent practically the whole day previously obtaining names for entries. Most of the men would not play. Eventually managed to collect a party to represent us. The great day came, and I was down to take part in 440, 880, and mile. The 880 was first on the list, and took the form of a relay, each string doing 880yds. The first offering in our team seized up after the first 440yds – tummy trouble. Although I felt slightly relieved (not being a ½ miler) I was annoyed, as I feel sure we'd have won it. I next met a very indignant Gnr who wanted to compete in the 440yds, so I gallantly stood back and let him take my place, and then felt furious because we came second, and each member got 5/-. Still, I'm not a sprinter. I was next in the high jump.

11 August. Darling, right in the middle of this I had to go out with Waggie. Took all afternoon and most of evening.

To continue where I left off. We jumped on wet grass in GYM SHOES! Consequently could not get a grip. I slipped and slithered as though I were on ice. We started at about 4'6", and I managed to clear 5'0". I must confess I did not feel at all safe, and could not relax to it, as I felt so unsafe on the grass. I began knocking the bar down at this height, I managed to clear 5'2" after a struggle and battle with a portion or two of my anatomy. Although I wore a little gadget to keep the "gentlemen" in order, one obstinate fellow would keep coming untucked at the most awkward moments, such as leaving the ground. For some unknown reason the six jumps I made from 5'0" upwards were all with the same results and I knocked it down with my bottom. Most annoying.

After many other odd events in the field and track - of which the tug-of-war was most outstanding, for the strained expressions if nothing else, and which we eventually won under the leadership of Jackie Evans – came the mile. I must admit I felt quite confident of being placed, and from the start adopted my usual tactic of running last for the first ¼ mile and gradually speeding up. The first ¼ mile was O.K., then I started up. I did not do too badly, but just could not get that little extra sprint and the race ended with me in one of the worst positions I can remember finishing in – I am certainly out of training. May have been the hangover of my leave!! And if that's what marriage does to you, I shall have to stick to being a husband, and not a miler.

The weather has been appalling recently. Although fine, you can lean against the wind.

No more now dearest, must post this.

Fondest love and adorations,

Ever you own, Johnnie.

Dover, 16 August 1942

Dearest Darling heart,

Will now make every effort to write this now delayed letter. Robbie and I spent the whole of yesterday afternoon in Folkestone, I going there with the intention of getting you the present as I told you on the phone. I got a list of jewellers in town, and systematically walked round. I was just getting desperate when we found a very nice shop, with only one or two rings on black velvet in the window. You know the idea. Really nice. I was rather amazed to find that they had any stock at all. Just as we went in the siren went, and the old bloke stood telling us all about the shortage of jewellery etc. We heard a plane, overhead. No one took any notice. It's quite usual to hear planes during sirens. Suddenly we heard that old familiar tearing noise, like slates sliding down a roof. It sounded uncomfortably near. Robbie ducked. I can't remember what I did. There followed four more. I kept feeling the next one was ours. They were coming quite near. 'Fraid we were not taking much notice. His assistant went on selling rings and I could hear him saying, "This is a very nice ring," in between each bomb. Everywhere I looked could see glass showcases, glass doors, a huge glass dome skylight, and mirrors. The plane(s?) was circling overhead, and the old boy said, "I should go into the street if I were you. They might machine gun!!" Robbie and I had some more shopping to do so, taking our lives in our hands, we braved the Luftwaffe onslaught, and went about our business. Pegs, I just don't know what to do, I went to every shop to get a charm, but there's nothing doing. So I'm afraid I have nothing for you at the moment. I'll get you something when I come home. Dearest, I do feel mean, but I have honestly tried so very hard.

17 August. Sorry for the break dear, but just as I was writing the above, we were subjected to shelling[54], don't know what was going on, but there must have been quite a lot of activity from the sound of things. Dearest, I felt the most miserable wretch in the world over your

---

[54] Dover was regularly shelled by German long range guns located in France.

present. I just feel fated. Hope the flowers arrived O.K. No more now dearest.

All my love,

Johnnie.

---

19 August 1942
Allies raid Dieppe.

Dover, 28 August 1942

Dearest Darling,

I feel a dreadful rat receiving all your dear letters without replying to any one of them. In spite of being kept busy I seem to have little to show for it, at least in a letter. It's awful really that I am unable to tell you about my week. Feel sure you appreciate this. Actually I've been quite busy, but not on boring type of work. It's all been most interesting really. I have spent several hours instructing on M/C.s etc. I have got to go out now with an officer. It's been grand stooging round on an M/C in shirt-sleeves in this weather.

Went for a swim yesterday at the impossible hour of 06.30hrs. Although I was very impressed with a bathe in the briny I was to encounter many snags. I had previously arranged with the cooks to have a jug of tea made for the party. When I got mine it was too sweet and only lukewarm. Still, it took the early morning taste out of my mouth. We had had a party in the mess the night before. This together with the heat gave me a thick head. I think I must have been still under the influence to have given my manly body to the waves at an hour when any intelligent persons are still abed. Eventually we got to the beach. I made the driver crawl along, as I could not bear the jolting of the vehicle. Destination reached I almost shied at the first fence, but realised my example must occasion nothing but praise from the men. But they beat me to it. I had just pulled my "shirt, Angola drab" over my head when a naked figure simply flashed past me. Now the part where we bathed was in view of W.R.N.S., A.T.S., etc., even if as I say they were in their beds – or perhaps someone else's. Still, it was "contrary to military discipline". The naked one sulked when ordered to cover his manly portions. I think he felt a certain amount of pride, for some unknown reason, in displaying himself. After all, from my point of view, there was nothing outstanding.

Just as I was negotiating a very careful line of attack on the briny, one of Goering's specials caused the sirens to be sounded. I had one of those ridiculous moments of wondering what was going to happen. I don't know if you ever experience these sorts of thoughts, but I imagined hoards of Stukas to come pouring out of nowhere and start a massed onslaught while I was in the H_2O. It did not come, and after crossing what seemed interminable paces of pebbles sharper than a bed of tin tacks - business end uppards – I took the plunge. It was then that I completely sobered up. I realised I was a fool to leave my bed. I "stooged" around for a while – longer than most – and once more staggered up to where my clothes had been left. I felt as though the tide had gone out to mid channel the distance I now had to walk. Undaunted, I circumnavigated more pebbles and needle like shingle I thought only existed in Brighton. We got back just in time for breakfast.

It was terribly hot here yesterday, and I felt like one great grease spot. I paid a visit to another of the sites[55] in the district during the morning, visited a Reception Station, and had a long talk with a rather "delightful" Medical Officer, and ended up engaging the local Constabulary in conversation with a query as to whether there was a swimming bath that I might teach Robbie and one or two of the others to swim. As I left them, they shouted at me in dreadful panic. Apparently I was going up a one way street coming down, or something equally odd. I gave a sickly grin, and meekly obeyed the law. They then went into detail to explain that one way streets were designed for traffic going in one direction. My reply was that I was going in one direction did not amuse them.

I stooged around our sites in the afternoon and nothing much occurred. Very quiet time lately. Managed to shut up shop quite early and went to bed feeling pleasantly tired. Lay in bed looking at my

---

[55] 349 Battery was also located at Hawkinge, site D11.

wife's photo for a while before turning out the light. I do miss her so very much. She is such a darling. And so here I am sending my love and fondest adorations,

Ever your own,

Johnnie.

Dover, 31 August 1942

My darling,

Well it's the last day of August '42, and another day nearer being home for good having I hope finished with war once and for all. Have been wondering what I should be doing now had it not been for the war. We should have had a nice little home and be just about beginning to get ourselves organised. But that certain gentleman decreed otherwise. I can only pray he never has a single dream or wish realised.

Was rather tickled to hear that my letters have become a prey of the merciless blue pencil[56]. Shall be glad if you'll tell me if I'm at all indiscrete as to get a bad mark.

Went out with Alex last night and he took me to a pub he'd found and which he raved about yesterday. Made me so thirsty that I decided I could resist the temptation no longer, so at 19.30hrs I washed and donned one blouse battle dress best, complete with shoes brown civilian type, trotted off with the man. I do not want to give too much away as I don't want the bloke in the censor department to come bursting in one night, but there is a pub which is patronised by a lady of, I should imagine, a very strong masculine desire. The first night Alex went there she did a naughty sort of can-can dance apparently. This involved the display of a large expanse of female limbs and that sort of thing, to say nothing of several coupons worth of pretties. It

---

[56] Letters were often opened, and censored where required, for security purposes.

appears that the only encouragement for this is a glass of stout and the feverish yells of rather unpleasantly minded soldiers. Of course, as may be imagined, this is contrary to all my ideals; but nevertheless, I went with Alex last night to see what he did get up to when he went out on his own. My disappointment on seeing the subject of the above was intense. She is devoid of looks, figure and personality. Perhaps I'm wrong when I say devoid of figure. Avoir du pois was most noticeable, and she seemed to bulge and swell in the most extraordinary places. There being no encouragement, either from the stout or piano, she retired to a previously fortified position taking with her some dreadful sandwiches, which she stuffed in her hand bag. Some young wag said he was "going to tell Mr Morrison about you!" And so I was not fortunate enough to see what has abstracted le Grand Alex and roused his manly desires. Nevertheless, we had a very enjoyable evening, gradually getting more and more confidential and sloppy as the alcoholic stimulants became more and more part of the blood stream. I expect my finger was jabbing harder and harder all evening, as I found myself nearly poking old A.'s eye out on one occasion. We did a steady little tour of the locals, and eventually ended up in another low dive. Fortunately this was only inhabited on our arrival by our own boys. The bus back was stiff with rather intoxicated soldiers all talking at once and all talking about different things.

The motorcycle instruction was very successful yesterday, and my pupil proved very much improved! I pottered about in the office most of the day, except for L.M.G.[57] lecture. Revolver practice in the afternoon. Feel Jerry has little to worry about when I go into action!!!

Everyone felt a little thick this morning after last night, and decided not to go swimming. Perhaps tomorrow. More L.M.G. lectures today. Visit from R.S.M. too, not very exciting news. Don't know why he comes.

It was Pop's birthday, managed to scribble something to him. He sent me some hair oil and cigarettes on Saturday. Most popular over the weekend with "Players". Can't get 'em in camp.

Take care of yourself for me. Fondest love darling,

Ever your own, Johnnie.

---

[57] Light machine gun.

Dover, 16 September 1942

My own darling sweetheart,

How I adore you for your sweet loveable letters. I have heard the poem several times before but never the chance to learn it. I'll endeavour to do so by the time I see you next.

While writing the above heard much crashing and thud-thud, bomp-bomp-rap-bomp-rap-bomp, so went to see what was to do. I feel someone was shelling someone, but could not quite make out who. Searchlights up here and over the other side. There appears to be a lot of air traffic over there. Their flak is making little orange pin-points in the sky. If only there was not so much beastliness to it it would be very beautiful. Have heard the drone of our own planes going somewhere, and much noise of flames. Went outside. What a sight! I should think Jerry had about 40 lamps in the air, and suddenly up from the ground went the most tremendous shower I've ever seen. At first it looked like golden rain. Red and yellow tracers weaving in and out of each other and the lamps. I saw a huge red flaming mass after the lights suddenly doused. It appeared perfectly stationary, but I was not in time to get the glasses on it. I'm afraid it was one of our lads "had it". How anything (within range) managed to keep up there for as long as he did before he was hit I cannot imagine. Perhaps the best simile I can give for the tracer was a steam engine shooting clouds of sparks into the air, with those huge icy fingers of the S/Ls[58] pointing accusingly into the night. More planes going over. Good luck boys. All the way along the coast as far as you can see the sky keeps reflecting orange splashes as the clouds catch the flash of the A.A. guns. Miles and miles away along the coast this is happening[59].

18 Sept. Well, well. Had so hoped to finish the above, but Maurice came in as I was writing. Just got back from leave, and told me the firing was getting more intense. Went out with him to see what was on

---

[58] Searchlights.
[59] 16/17 September 1942, 369 aircraft of Bomber Command, including aircraft from the training group, attacked Essen and other targets in Germany.

and the alarm went. When it was over, came back about 01.30hrs. Felt so tired I went to bed hoping to finish next morning. Was awakened early by an officer who wanted some ammunition for range practice. Why not tell me before? No! Wait till last thing.

I'm doing Jackie's job this week as he's on leave. Have more or less given up mine for the time being. Spent all day yesterday exchanging clothing and kit. Thoroughly enjoyed it for the change, but most tiring. You might have thought we were the 50/- tailors the way people groused – still, I think I can honestly say there's not a single man without he's thoroughly equipped with good and serviceable kit.

19 Sept. Yet another day. Oh! Hell. It does make yer mad. 'Fraid I've got some bad news dear. It looks like the 23ʳᵈ is off. Same reason as last time. Why oh why can't I be allowed to have just ONE leave without having it put off like this. Wanted on the phone now. Damn. Damn. Damn.

Later. Two seconds thought on his part and he could have found it all out on his own. Now I'm going to finish this letter and am taking time off this afternoon to write to my wife. She does deserve a letter, so "dash 'em all".

To go back to where I left off I just do not know when I shall get my leave. Had so hoped that this time all would be OK. Of course it may turn out alright even yet. But I loathe the uncertainty. It must be wretched for you. Perhaps now the time is not so far away when I shall be able to come home every night.

No more now. All my fondest love and adorations,

Ever your own,

Johnnie.

Dover, 21 September 1942

Sweetest darling,

Thank you from the bottom of my heart for that cake which has just arrived. I have not yet made an attack on it, but the recce appeared to be most satisfactory. I'm going to be right down mean and keep it all to myself. If only I had not had to send that last letter of mine. Still, I suppose I'm lucky so far to have been able to be so near home and see you so often. As yet there is no more news. Rumours of course are prolific.

Robbie and I finished quite early on Saturday evening and came back to the mess and read. During the evening, while we were nice and quiet in front of the fire our bombers started going over[60]. I've never heard such a noise. Shook the buildings. It was just one incessant roar. We went outside – can't think why now – to see what we could see. It was dark, and although we waited for ages we saw nothing except searchlight and flak on t'other side. Later in the evening the huts shook after some terrific explosions. No one seems to know where they came from, but it was something going down, or being blown up. You could almost see the huts shake.

Went to bed nice and early on Saturday, and slept like a top until about 08.45hrs on Sunday! Jackie back on Sat. night, so have relinquished my share in that department now. Am rather glad, for – as you may imagine – they are terribly busy at the moment.

Had a letter from Tich last week. Don't think I told you. His Squadron Leader had said that he did not want him to partake in night ops yet, and so Tich asked him if he could have four days off, and he got it!

Yesterday was a typical English Sunday. Rained all day and again today. Wish I'd had my mac. Am still trying to get all my stuff packed up to send home. Can't think how to get the case home. It has no lock on it. Must devise some scheme or other.

---

[60] Raids on the night of 20-21 September targeted Saarbrücken, bombed by 118 aircraft, and Munich, bombed by 89 aircraft.

Robbie and I went down for a drink last night. Felt a bit depressed before we went. Met a couple of officers down there. Had a pleasant chinwag and returned feeling much better. To bed early again. Slept until 08.45 again today. Can't think what's wrong. Seem to feel so tired all the time. Spent this morning indoors as it rained so much. Hope to finish early tonight, and do my packing for sending home.

Well my dearest, all my love and cuddles. Think of you so much these days.

Ever your very own adoring husband,

Johnnie.

Dover[61], 10 October 1942

My darling,

As you suspected I have just returned from the "flap doodle" during which it was absolutely impossible to write[62]. You know by now, as I do of you, that I write whenever I can, and also how sorry I feel.

Now, first of all dearest, how grateful I am for your letters. What a great ray of sunshine you are my sweet. I am so lucky to have such a dear wife.

Let me now try to give you all the gen since I last wrote to you. We had notice that it was definitely coming off the morning before it actually started. You have no idea how much there is to do.

13 October. The first abortive effort having gone wildly awry, I am now going to write this letter today or burst, and since I do not intend to perform the latter act, I have the feeling that summat will not get done

---

[61] 349 B.H.Q. relocated from Farthingloe to Acrise Place, north of Dover, on 26 September.
[62] An eight day exercise centred in the Ashdown Forest.

as a result. But still I MUST write you dearest. I had another dear letter today. Read it so eagerly. I'm longing to know what's happening. Keep thinking about you. I cannot seem to think of you as two, and I love you both so very much. Do please keep me very much in touch. That little butterfly is so precious to me. Please take extra care of him for me.

Perhaps my best plan is to start from the beginning of the exercise and work up to date. I started telling you about all the work I had to do before it started. As can be imagined, it was fairly heavy. Loading vehicles was quite a day's job on its own. Some bright youth had left something off when I came to check it over, which resulted in the whole thing being unpacked again. It had to go right at the back!

We kicked off at some unearthly hour before bats had gone to roost, or the new day was more than a blur in the sky. My eyes were heavy with sleep, and I felt grouchy. Not unusual these days. One always finds things not quite so without looking for them. I had one of those mornings when I did not get on too well with my razor, and went on parade with dried patches of blood (for those who could see them). The start was however well to time and quite according to schedule, and being a fine dry morning I felt much better. I sat quite snugly in my vehicle and let my thoughts roam. We went though some beautiful country, and I eventually could not resist singing. Fortunately my driver has no more idea of music (!!!) than I, and we sang away quite happily. I felt one or two pangs of gloom seeing the autumnal colours of the woods and forests, but these colours were really wonderful. One last big show before the fall….. and then I remembered spring would follow, and then summer, and then…

14 October. Had to leave this after I'd written the above. Usual interruption. Charges to be dealt with. Makes me mad. Last evening I had to go on a map reading exercise with some officers. Was pitch dark, and all the roads looked the same. Caused a certain amount of tension trying to select the roads when travelling at speed, and my driver drove like the wind. It was also a sort of race to get back first. We had one break at a country pub half way round. It was cold last night too. Got back at 23.30hrs. Felt tired and ready for bed.

Ever your own, Johnnie, Britain, 1938-42

Supposed to go on a route march today. Can't see how I can manage it as I have so much to do here. You'll smile perhaps, but I feel very cross about it.

Let me tell you about the exercise now. Having started off at dawn, or before, we had gone quite a long way by 11.30hrs, and were beginning to feel very hungry. Went through much orchard country, and at halts were given some glorious apples, pears, and plums. The vehicle which I was in managed to pull up next to a cottage at another halt, and some dear soul gave us tea, bread and butter, apples, and plums. It really was most welcome, especially as our next meal was not until 16.00hrs. Did that go down well too. My favourite steak and onions! In the field too! Darkness came, and then bed in the back of a lorry, sleeping on a 4ft table. Slept like a log, to be woken at 02.30hrs and told we were moving "immediate" (in block letters) repeat "immediate". Usual excitement of finding things in the pitch black and waking sleeping and cursing soldiers. It was raining hard when we started off, and the vehicles were sliding "crabwise" out of the night's roost. Made a strange sight. It rained nearly all morning. It's a miserable pastime sitting in a vehicle watching the rain splash against the windscreen and miles of wet road in front of you. Besides which we were wet from the night before, not to say hungry and sleepy (that incidentally seemed to be the only discomfort, sleep and hunger). We reached our destination about 18.00hrs, and fell ravenously on the meal. Followed by much spending of pennies in the bushes, and – a luxury – a wash and shave in our mess tins. Felt much better after that. We were in a huge wood with very tall trees, mostly beech. The sun kept trying to push sheaves of yellow light into the dark interior, but the rain won, and the heavens let everything drop. The trees made matters worse – although it sounds impossible – and it was too much for the leaves to hold the amount of water off us. Result, every place where people were sleeping was soaked. Even the lorries inside where people dripped all over you.

I had, what now seems, a very amusing incident in the night. Poor old bladder, extended to its full, had to be answered, and I had to climb over six sleeping bodies in the pitch dark. I managed to avoid all except the last two, the first of whom received the business end of a hob nailed boot in the middle of square four. He yelled (don't blame him) so loud that I jumped and put my other boot right in the second blokes open mouth. After extracting myself I jumped down from the tailboard

112

of the lorry and landed on what I thought was firm ground. It was
before the rain, but it now took on the resemblance of a skating rink
and I went for six face downwards in the muddy tracks of vehicles.
Grinding my teeth with fists clenched I extricated myself from the
intricacies of camouflage netting. It was so dark that by now I was
completely lost that I could not see the edge of the wood, the sky
above, a star, the moon – absolute blackness everywhere. I was so
cross with myself, and the tree stumps and trees themselves added to
my fury. Rain was pelting down. Why I should be such a gentleman as
to go for miles in the dark to spend a penny with all that water already
coming down I can't imagine. Having I'm afraid gone the distance I
could contain myself no longer, and relieved myself against what later
transpired to be the O.C.'s car. Still, what the ----! The return journey
to my lorry would have been impossible but for the very able assistance
of the guard. Hearing my plight, one of them challenged me. I had not
noticed his approach, and I must admit I was startled by his challenge.
Eventually reached bed and slept about an hour to be woken with the
move again.

The next day was a repetition of the day before, and the next, except
that we returned on that day. I had to do escort to a "lame" lorry home
with M/C. Developed gear trouble about 23.30hrs, and loaded said
M/C on said "lame" lorry. Took over control of this vehicle –
suffering from broken feed pipe (the lorry, not me!) and with a
flickering torch and the aid of a map that had become almost
unreadable owing to being soaked, proceeded to direct the vehicle
back. We had about 90 miles to go. The map was at its worst and the
torch hardly visible at a very tricky part of the road. Met a Canadian
returning from leave about 23.59hrs, and asked the way to nearest
town called 'X'. He thought it was "along that road there". It later
transpired that "that road there" led into a very muddy farmyard, and
much excitement was experienced in getting it out. Nothing daunted,
we then travelled on a star and eventually struck a main road, and
managed to find a landmark or two on the map, and realised where we
were. All the time the top speed of the vehicle was about 15 mph, and
on hills never more than 2 mph. Eyes kept dozing off. Road was now
very dirty, and the open front made things quite cold. Then we struck a
Home Guard detachment on the duty of guarding a road block. They
simply pounced on our vehicle like hawks, rifles, bayonets, red lamps,

revolvers, and torches. Everyone in turn shouted, "Halt! Who goes there?" Next they wanted to see my pass. I said I was not on leave (as though I'd take a lorry out at that time of the day – approx 03.30hrs now – looking as I did, mud up to the eyebrows, no shave, and they thought I was on leave). I then showed them my identification papers etc. which were taken into their Captain. The little man who took them vanished for about ½ an hour. When he returned I feel sure I smelt whisky, so supposed they'd had a drink whilst reading my docs. We next encountered the H.G. at the other end of the road, who seemed unable to understand how I'd got in. I then went into long detail to explain that I'd been let in at the other end after my docs etc. had been checked. Apparently it was alright, and "George" was detailed to "jump on the running board and take these chappies" through the next barrier. Poor George must have had a long walk back after he left us. At about 05.00hrs, I could keep awake no longer, and put Maurice (who was with me) in charge and the second driver at the wheel. We arrived back about 08.30hrs feeling very tired, wet, and hungry. I then had a bath, change, and did a little shooting in the woods nearby with Maurice. Reveille had been put at 12.00hrs, but we felt if we went to sleep we'd feel more tired than if we kept awake. Went to bed about 21.30hrs. I got up at 06.00hrs next morning and went shooting again. It's a new game here with me to go to bed early, and go shooting in the morning. Have felt much better for it too. Have shot three or four rabbits, and made some very good suppers too. Had them braised with onions, and chopped carrots and turnips. It was glorious.

Well my darling, I seem to have made it so far. Rather long winded perhaps – hope I've not bored you! I can't say when I'll be home on leave yet, we have more exercises next week. Will try to drop you a line or two then. I'll write in the meantime.

Can you let me have the gloves and pullover as soon as possible. I shall need those next week. Well my dearest, must close now. Do please let me know all the news as and when you can, even if I don't write to you at times.

All my fondest love,

Ever your own adoring,

Johnnie.

Dover, 15 October 1942

Dearest,

Had no letter today, so am still in suspense to know what is happening. Every minute of the day I have been thinking of you and wondering what you were doing. Have now put your photo on my desk so that I can cheer myself up when things appear rather impossible. I am now looking forward to a photo of you and Nickie together. That will be a great thrill for me.

Have been quite uneventfully busy today, so have finished quite early. I think I'll go to bed early. Had a letter from Tich, sent his love to you. He seems to be unable to give me any details, and I am unable to give him any. Waggie has taken himself off on 48hrs once again, so his length is missing from the office just now.

I was rather late getting to the pay table today and Old Alex got his own back on me by paying me in sixpences! As I said, it was everything barring the jam jars.

I went out for an hour's walk with a gun tonight. Saw nothing but a few woodpigeon. Had a couple of shots "on the wing", but it's very difficult catching them like that. I passed through several fields of sheep and cows. It made me laugh to see their expressions when they saw me. One sheep stared at me and stopped chewing to see what I was doing. Apparently I was OK as they went on chewing, watching me out of the corner of their eyes. Wish you'd been there.

Have no more now, and will now go to bed.

All my fondest love dearest,

Ever adoringly,

Your own,

Johnnie.

---

23 October 1942
Second battle of El Alamein begins.

Dover, 30 October 1942

Dearest,

After the wild and hectic life of the exercise, we return to perhaps an even wilder and more hectic time here. It must seem an awfully uninteresting letter writer these days when I at least do write to you. It's almost impossible to give any real news these days.

The scheme as a whole was very successful if the results handed down from higher authority are any guide. I will say what I saw appeared very satisfactory. It took place over quite a large area[63]. If it was any experience we had all sorts of weather imaginable, from bright sunshine to cold winds. Our "home" for the eight days was the back of a lorry which during the day time was a swarm of people using it as an office. My bed was a 4'0" table on which I slept like a log. Reveille was at 05.00hrs invariably, and we finally got to bed about 23.30hrs, so needed no rocking when we got our heads down. The day was normally taken up with office routine in the field or with moves. I'll give fuller details in my next letter. Some amusing incidents occurred, but I'm rather rushed at the moment to go into details.

You will be amused to hear that your husband drove an 8cwt lorry for eighty miles without a stop. What was more it meant double de-clutching and after the first mile or two I did not crash a single gear. I was complimented on it afterwards, and no one apparently knew I'd not driven before.

Well dearest, I have to pay the battery out today, and collect the money at 10.00hrs. Darling, I've missed you. I'm striving as hard as I can to get leave. It's a very difficult job just now. I must say things look,

---

[63] An eight day exercise held in Ashdown Forest.

perhaps, a little brighter, but everyone else is in the same boat, and still unable to get theirs. Still, that's no reason why I should not get mine.

Fondest love for now,

Ever your own,

Johnnie.

---

8 November 1942
First 'Operation Torch' landings take place of the Allied Forces invasion of French North Africa.

Dover, 12 November 1942

My very own darling,

    Thank you once again for the wonderful leave dearest. That leave will always stand out in my memory and will cheer me in my blue moods which I never seem to be able to shake off. It seems incredible that the leave is now over, still I suppose that we must make the most of things now and keep smiling.

The train journey back proved to be very uneventful, except that the carriage was very full. I gather that I was very lucky to get a seat. You will have already gathered that the train stopped at London Bridge. It is always a thankless task trying to get into a blacked out compartment, and that one was no exception. I found myself tripping over all sorts of humanity.

When I got to this end I was just in time to get a good shelling. I was quite glad when the car arrived to take me out of it.

I seem to have been dogged by rather nasty minded gremlins since I got back, and they induced Robbie to go on leave just when I got back. Also Waggie, so all that is left here is a rather mystified man and one or two others in the same boat so it now means that there are several strange looking people endeavouring to find out what is happening.

Everything seems very much the same at the moment, and there are no further reports at the time of going to press.

I have had some rather unfortunate news on coming back, when Alex tells me that there is only a couple of bob to come this week, and that I also have a telephone bill of 11/- to pay. Would it be asking too much of you to beg a £1? It seems I am not in quite such good straits in the financial line as I had hoped.

I am sorry that this is so miserably short, but there is quite a lot to do, and I shall have to start it soon. Will you please thank Mother and Father for all they did for me to make it such a wonderful leave. I shall be writing them in the morning I hope. I will also write you more fully then I hope. No more now dearest darling. All my very fondest love and adorations. Remember that wherever I may be, I shall always be thinking of you. I took a good look at the Pole star last night[64], and wondered how the dance was going. Hope you enjoyed it dear.

Ever your own,

Johnnie.

Dover, 14 November 1942

My very dearest sweetheart,

Many thanks for the letter you sent me yesterday. Sorry not to write yesterday as I had hoped. It seems the gremlins are entirely unfavourable towards my letter writing. I must oust them once and for all. They suddenly thrust some very unexpected work in my way so that I could not wriggle out of it, in consequence of which I could not write you. Still, let's try now. Started the above in the mess, but the noise was too much. There seems to be a great state of excitement and jubilation everywhere. I must admit everyone seems most cheerful. It's

---

[64] John and Peggy had an agreement to look at the Pole star wherever they were and think of each other.

most gratifying. Here's hoping it may continue so until the end of the war, and this time no set backs.

I paid out with Alex yesterday, and on the way to the bank he told me how much he and Marjorie had enjoyed the evening out. I rather believe it was a very pleasant change for them both.

16 November. Yet once more I'll try to finish this letter. In spite of the amount of work at present on hand, I have surprisingly little news to give of real interest value.

Have just received your registered letter, for which I'm very grateful. I'll write Mother and thank her. I feel very guilty and a little awkward about accepting it. Are you in agreement with this method of getting money?

We have had a mess "smoker" here tonight, so expect there will be one or two hangovers tomorrow.

Well dearest, there's no more now. Please look after you for me.

All my fondest love,

Ever your own,

Johnnie.

Dover, 17 November 1942

Dearest,

Many thanks for your letter, just received. I suppose that we are getting near the time when you can let me have some news. I do so hope you can give it me soon and that it's all for the best.

Today I am in possession of some news which rather goes beyond my wildest dreams. I had to go into R.H.Q. with Waggie this morning. When we got back from the "smoker" I was in a comfortable state of inebriation and was greeted by the duty clerk saying I had to go into

Ever your own, Johnnie, Britain, 1938-42

R.H.Q. by 08.15hrs. It was a curse really, as I had rather hoped for a
lie-in after such an evening. All the same, I managed to get out of bed
onto my feet today and was surprised that I felt no ill effects from the
night before. After an awful breakfast I accompanied the great white
cheese into R.H.Q. No one seemed to know what this was all about. I
went complete with voluminous notebook and pencils, and was told to
"wait there for a minute or two" which I did. "There" turned out to be
the draughtiest hall I yet have had the fortune to stand in. One or two
other officers arrived, and after much clicking of heels and saluting,
they asked me into the room where I presumed the conference was to
be held – or whatever it was. I was kept waiting there for about an
hour, and then Waggie came out and very mysteriously beckoned me
into the room and closed the door after me. Then in a hushed whisper,
and husky voice told me that the R.S.M. was being discharged by the
M.O. and that at this conference it had been decided that I should fill
the vacancy. My first impression was of being completely lost for
words. Can't think why, but these sorts of things take my breath away,
and I "come over all silly" and lost for words. After this I was ushered
into a room full of officers who repeated what Waggie had said. Now it
remains as to whether records approve it. Apart from leaving the lads –
which would be an awful wrench – I cannot see any drawbacks. The
pay situation will certainly help. I believe this will show quite a good
increase. It's still in the air at the moment. To be quite honest I
sincerely hope it comes off. I do feel though that if it doesn't go
through I have been honoured by even being considered by the
Officers of the Regiment.

If it does come off I shall feel really tickled pink – I am then called
"Mr" by one and all.

Pegsie, I should not mention this to Mother and Pop. I suppose that
the temptation will be very great, but I should be very grateful if you
could resist it until you know it's OK. I feel very much bucked about
all this. You can imagine me hobnobbing with the Colonel if it comes
through. Still we mustn't count our chickens until they're hatched.

The "smoker" last night was a great success. We started about
18.15hrs, and finished about 23.00hrs. Beer was ordered by the gallon!
We had a separate room to ourselves, there being about twenty of us.
We sang most of the time, and in spite of the alcohol purchased and

consumed we all returned quite sober. At any rate I was able to return at my own pace and under my own steam with the rest.

We have had photographs taken today. I'll get some and send you when available, if they are not too expensive.

Well my dearest heart, no more now except my very fondest love and adorations. I'm thinking of you at all times.

Ever your own loving husband,

Johnnie.

Dover, 19 November 1942

Hello Adorable,

Well, well. Here's your own little pink haired lil' boy once again, and this time with perhaps the best news I have ever been able to give you. Do you remember what I said in my last letter about moving my abode at the same time as receiving promotion? I'm happy to tell you today that this has been approved by Records. All I now await is the official posting. I came into Regt today for keeps, so next time you write, will you leave off the other designation, and just show the Regt. The rank is still the same until you hear to the contrary. I'll send you a wire when I'm officially ensconced. In the meantime I am only "acting", and until the other bloke goes, am being shepherded around and shown the sights etc. I have not yet realised the true magnitude of the whole affair. It really is rather mystifying, and I'm still in a great whirl.

I felt an awful heartbreak today when I said goodbye to all the lads. Really made me feel sad. Fortunately I do know them nearly all here, and although the new job is strange, it is far simpler than the other one. I must confess that it is now realising something I never thought it possible to attain. Just sit back and think what this will mean in rank and responsibility. It's absolutely the highest I can get and the pay!! It will be more than a great many people we know who walk about in nice uniforms!

Ever your own, Johnnie, Britain, 1938-42

I once said I would not aim for this position and might not take it if I were offered it. I'd be a B.F. if I didn't accept. I'm just sweating now on the top line waiting for the official confirmation to come through. I'd like to see Pop's face when he hears about it. I have a consolation too in coming here, Alex is also being posted at a later date, so it's not going to be so lonely as I first thought.

I have very little other news at the moment dear, and am expecting to be called for an interview at any moment, so think I'll close while I've got the chance.

For the time being dearest, your pink haired husband sends you all his fondest love and adorations. Is there any news of our Nickie yet?

All my love darling heart,

Ever your own loving husband,

Johnnie.

Dover, 20 November 1942

My darling,

Am feeling sad that I have not yet had a letter today, or yesterday. I expect it's gone to the other address. Days seem so empty and sad at the moment in spite of the new position, especially as you can imagine at a time like this. I still feel nearly broken hearted at having to leave my boys. I really did love them so, and they were so good. This crowd have been desperately spoiled. There seems to be no discipline whatever. It's going to be an uphill struggle, and it's just at a time when I don't want it either. There are plenty of other things to do without having to clear up after someone's sloppiness. That's all it amounts to. When I think what these people used to be like. They've been ruined. I can see quite a lot of answers to all the trouble we've had in the past now. There's quite a lot for me to do during the day. I now discover that the "other bloke" did not even have a desk in the office. Heavens, I must know what's going on. 'Fraid I shall not meet with approval in the methods to be used, but I just can't help it. It's got to be done in the way that I want it.

Last night was of course an excuse for everyone to sting me for a drink. It will be O.K. when this actually comes through and I get my back pay, but it's 'ard on a bloke now. You'll find the old allowance will bump up a hell of a lot. It will be quite a nice little packet now. Do you know, I have been seriously wondering if I would be wise to sign on for keeps now having reached this status. The position carries a host of advantages in peacetime. I think I'll look into the matter very thoroughly.

Have spent today being "run-in" and start on my own officially tomorrow. Inspections etc. Should not be too difficult. By the way, did I tell you Jackie Evans has now taken my old job. He's thrilled to bits about it too. Since writing the above, I have been down to see if there was a letter for me, but have not been able to find one.

Well my dearest, no more now, except fondest love and adorations. Please look after yourself,

Ever adoringly,

Johnnie.

22 November 1942 *(assumed Dover)*

My own darling,

Sorry I've not written before this weekend. I have an important date with Clair[65] and I can't say when I shall be able to write to you next. Must just leave a letter before I see her. I'll write to you as

---

[65] This letter differs considerably from other letters before or after this date, being plainly very rushed, and written on a page torn from a notebook. A cryptic list written in Peggy's handwriting on the reverse of a letter from John to Peggy in September 1942 notes the following, "Clair Mica: Caucasus, Libya, W.Africa, India, Russia. Madagascar, Iceland, Ceylon, Arabia." From this it can be surmised that 'Clair' was a pre-agreed code for 76th H.A.A. Regt being sent abroad to one of the defined countries, in this case 'W.Africa'.

soon as I can dearest heart. By the time you get this I shall most likely know all about what she has been wanting me for for such a long time. She's an awkward b----. Had hoped to phone you today, but it's been impossible. I've been rushed to bits as you can imagine in order to meet the a/m[66] lady in time. Darling, will you please tell my mother. I just can't explain it all to her.

Must rush darling heart. Please look after you both for me. I adore you more than anything in life. God bless you and look after you for me my angel darling.

Yours for ever adoringly,

Your very own husband,

Johnnie.

P.S. Will you please tell my Ma & Pa I just haven't had a second to write. I will as early as possible. JK.

---

23 November 1942
76th H.A.A. Regt R.A. entrains for Glasgow.

24 November 1942
76th H.A.A. Regt R.A. embarks transport ships *Batory* and *Durban Castle*, Glasgow.

27 November 1942
Convoy sets sail from the Firth of Clyde.

6 December 1942
Regiment disembarks, Algiers.

---

[66] Aforementioned.

John's war in context

Prelude, the pre war years

John Kemp joined the Territorial Army (T.A.) in 1938, as did many at that time, in response to the mounting threat to peace in Europe caused by Hitler's expansionist politics. The regiment[67] of which he was now a member was a heavy anti-aircraft (H.A.A.) unit. It was originally formed during 1922 and was based at Mill Hill, London, where weekly T.A. training was undertaken, augmented by annual camps for live gunnery practice.

The British Government had been reluctant during the mid to latter part of the 1930's to commit budgets to developing and arming the military despite the growing power of Germany's armed forces. However, the recognition of the potential that the Luftwaffe could bomb Britain early in any war, particularly in view of the bombing that had occurred during the Spanish Civil War, gave impetus to the need for and development of new anti-aircraft measures. At the heart of this was the need to upgrade the current issue of anti-aircraft gun, existing equipment being of First World War vintage and unable to counter large numbers of the modern fast flying aircraft now in service with the German Luftwaffe.

---

[67] 53rd (City of London) Anti-Aircraft Regiment, R.A. (T.A.), comprising 157th, 158th (City of London), 159th (Lloyd's), Btys, this being part of 1st Anti-Aircraft Division.

Heavy anti-aircraft gun defences during World War I initially used modified 13 pounder Royal Horse Artillery guns against the enemy aircraft flying over British trenches, and the Zeppelin and German Gotha bomber raids carried out over Britain. These were later developed into more powerful 3" calibre guns, these becoming the standard issue to H.A.A. batteries. In the decade after World War I there was little significant development of anti-aircraft guns, this being restricted principally to the modification of some existing 3" guns to provide mobility by the fitting of trailer mountings. Those at T.A. units however, as noted by John Kemp in his training experience, remained as static or semi mobile mountings dating from World War I. It was not until the early 1930's that the need to replace the 3" guns with a device more capable of dealing with higher and faster flying aircraft was finally recognised, together with the need for this to be mobile. A specification was developed and issued by the Director of Artillery, a new 3.7" QF (quick firing)[68] gun being prototyped from this by Vickers in 1934, and subsequently, after modification, going into initial manufacture in 1936. By 1937 the new 3.7" Vickers H.A.A. gun[69] had completed the necessary trials and production been instructed, but the first deliveries did not commence until 1938, and then only in small quantities. By September 1938 just 480 guns had been delivered compared with a requirement for 1,260, a number that was to be subsequently increased. To meet the shortfall 450 existing First World War 3" guns were brought back into service, approximately 200 of these having previously been modernised.

In parallel with the development of the anti-aircraft gun during World War I was the recognised need to be able to engage aircraft as moving targets with greater accuracy. The success of hitting an aircraft in flight rests simplistically upon the ability to predict an aircraft's future position relative to the trajectory of the shell, this taking account of the aircraft's height, speed and course, the arc of flight of the artillery round fired, and the prevailing weather conditions. Equipment, aptly called a Predictor, was developed to compute these variables based on

---

[68] QF guns used ammunition in which the shell round was combined with a brass cartridge charge as one item for quick loading and firing, rather than the alternative of charge and shell as two separate elements.
[69] See Appendix 2 for details.

visual observation through a telescope of the target aircraft's course, but was limited to aircraft flying below 25,000ft. The equipment could calculate the future intercept position of an aircraft and the round fired through assessment of altitude, course and the rate of angular change of the target, this being achieved prior to World War II by means of clockwork and electro mechanical systems. This information was then transmitted over cables from the Predictor to the gun and interpreted by the detachment manning the gun. The use of H.E. shells exploding in the proximity of the aircraft was the preferred ammunition to destroy or damage the aircraft, shrapnel shells being found less effective except against low flying planes, the timing of the shell's fuze being determined by the Predictor.

Early Predictor systems were limited to being usable only against visual targets. The development of radio, however, had created an understanding by the 1930's that short wave radio waves were disrupted and reflected by passing aircraft. Interest from Government led to the funding and development of this phenomenon into what was to be called RADAR (RAdio Detection And Ranging), providing an ability to both 'see' aircraft at night and in poor visibility, and, importantly, at significant distances, vital in providing early warning of attack. Initially radar was developed to provide strategic early warning, this being accomplished by the construction from 1936 onwards of monitoring stations that eventually covered the coastline from Cornwall to Shetland, known as Chain Home. Whilst this provided forewarning of approaching raids, in itself it did not provide any greater accuracy in anti-aircraft gunfire. It was thus a logical step for radar to be developed at a tactical scale and integrated with Predictor equipment, the first units, called Ground Laying radar (G.L.), being issued to some H.A.A. batteries in late 1939. This continued to be developed throughout the war, being fitted to searchlights as well as being supplied to all A.A. gun batteries. Mobile radar units became available by the time of the landings in Sicily in 1943. Such was the sophistication of radar by the end of the war that systems in use with A.A. guns deployed in a field role were able to identify incoming mortar rounds and the position from which these had been fired, allowing counter measures to be taken. This same sophistication also provided a high level of accuracy in intercepting and destroying V1 flying bombs in flight by H.A.A. fire, in conjunction with the newly introduced anti-aircraft shell proximity fuzes in 1944.

The development of Light Anti-aircraft (L.A.A.) guns after World War I was tardy, it being believed that conventional machine guns would suffice in this role. It was not until 1936 that it was recognised that heavier calibre rapid firing guns would be required to counter the threat of dive bombers and low flying aircraft at close quarters. The gun identified to fulfil this role and that came into use with L.A.A. units was the mobile mounted Bofors 40mm L.A.A. gun, capable of firing 120 high explosive rounds per minute.

Alongside the requirement to upgrade equipment in the 1930's was the need for trained men to operate the guns and associated equipment, together with a rationalisation of the existing A.A. organisation. Recruiting to the T.A. for Anti-aircraft defence began in earnest after 1936, together with the conversion of some infantry T.A. units to A.A. roles, resulting in A.A. defence being manned below H.Q. level staff solely by T.A. troops. In 1938 the A.A. role was split into Light Anti-aircraft and Heavy Anti-aircraft designations these being identified as regiments falling under the auspices of Air Defence Great Britain (A.D.G.B.). By 1939 A.A. defences were managed by Fighter Command from sector control rooms, these being able to provide information on approaching raids whilst also coordinating and controlling appropriate action of guns and searchlights in conjunction with the interception by R.A.F. fighters.

The shortfall in H.A.A. equipment, which persisted into 1943, hindered training of T.A. regiments, some, as with John's 158 Battery, being on outdated equipment, whilst access to live firing was restricted due to the shortage of suitable practice ranges. New gunnery ranges were opened in response, including Weybourne, Norfolk, where 158 Battery undertook training in 1938. Live firing practice consisted of shooting at a target sleeve towed at some distance behind a tug aircraft. Whilst this was valuable experience for the gun detachments, the target travelled on a straight and level course at constant speed, whereas enemy aircraft could well change course, speed, and altitude to avoid anti-aircraft fire.

Hitler's annexation of Austria followed by Germany's demands for Sudetenland autonomy in Czechoslovakia prompted Prime Minister Neville Chamberlain to meet with Hitler on 13 September 1938. Meetings over the following days culminated on 30 September with one between Chamberlain, Daladier (Prime Minister of France), Hitler, and Mussolini and the signing of the Munich Agreement. During this period, however, T.A. regiments were mobilised from 23 September 1938 under a State of Emergency due to concerns about imminent war, with approximately 50,000 troops being deployed in a little over 24 hours. Twenty-four A.A. regiments were located in parks and open space around London, including the 53rd City of London Regiment, John's Regiment, at Sheen Gate, Richmond Park. All troops were subsequently stood down by 14 October 1938.

Lessons were learnt and weaknesses recognised from this mobilisation, resulting in the raising of requirements for A.A. strength, together with restrictions being lifted on recruiting that had previously been in place. It was also recognised that integration of operations between the R.A.F. and A.A. was necessary to provide a coordinated approach to air defence, ultimate command of A.D.G.B. being given to Fighter Command.

Artillery training was soon brought under Royal Artillery Training Establishment to cope with the numbers of raw recruits being enlisted, firstly through the Military Training Act of 1939, and then the National Service (Armed Forces) Act that made all men between the ages of 18 and 41 liable for conscription, training centres being opened in every command area.

Britain, 1938-42

Mounting tension in Europe and the seeming inevitability of war with Germany as the year of 1939 progressed led to T.A. anti-aircraft units being mobilised on 21 August and troops called up for active service. War was formally declared on 3 September following Germany's invasion and occupation of Poland on 1 September. John along with others from 158 Battery had been posted to 282 Battery of 88th H.A.A. Regiment on 21 April 1939, the regiment, as with 53rd, being based at White City and being part of 26th A.A. Brigade. They were fully incorporated into 88th Regiment on 30 September.

Gun sites were rapidly deployed around London, many in emplacements constructed by troops using sandbags, and with troop shelters in some instances built from straw bales and tarpaulins. John was deployed first at Hurlingham Polo Ground[70] as part of London's Inner Artillery Zone (I.A.Z.) defences. The Regiment subsequently relocated within the I.A.Z. to Lewis gun positions in north London to defend 'Vulnerable Points' (V.P.s) at munitions factories in Enfield and Waltham Abbey, all sites being controlled from a central operations room at Brompton. Gun sites at this time used sound locators to identify the positions of enemy aircraft, as Ground Laying radar was not yet generally available. Lewis gun positions were a common feature at gun positions early in the war to augment the limited number of

---

[70] Gun site reference ZW8. See Appendix 1 for gun site map references and locations.

heavy guns available.

A British Expeditionary Force landed in France on 12 September 1939, and was reinforced over the next eight months to total ten divisions, little conflict taking place. On 10 May 1940 the Phoney War, as the period between September and May became known, came to an end with Germany's invasion of the low countries and France, Allied troops being forced back from the German French border to the Channel coast in two weeks. With the real threat of encirclement and capture, an emergency evacuation of troops began from Dunkirk and nearby beaches, commencing in earnest on 27 May and lasting until 4 June. During this time 338,226 troops were rescued, many being brought back to Britain in numerous small craft that had been pressed into service, but leaving much of the troops' equipment abandoned in France. John's Regiment had been preparing for overseas service immediately prior to this date (this following a previously cancelled mobilisation during April) and was in transit to and preparation for boarding ships at Southampton as the evacuation commenced. Due to the deteriorating situation in France, the embarkation was abandoned, the Regiment being immediately returned to the I.A.Z., John's battery being deployed at Annerly Park[71] near Crystal Palace.

In France, the government had left Paris for the south ahead of the German advance. With France falling into German hands, Churchill was anxious to prevent the French fleet from being taken over and used by the German navy, with its resultant potential to further threaten North Atlantic convoys supplying Britain. He therefore considered, in conjunction with the French, assembling a further British Expeditionary Force (B.E.F.) to counter this. It was in response to this that the 88th H.A.A. Regiment received a further instruction to mobilise on 4 June, guns being taken out of action on their sites on 8 June before moving once again to Southampton on 11 June, where equipment was loaded onto waiting ships, these setting sail for Brest. Meanwhile the Regiment's troops were moved to Plymouth for boarding on 14 June. Churchill had, meanwhile, sent General Alan Brooke to France for a meeting with French officials on 13 June, during which it became plain that sending further forces to France

---

[71] Gun site reference ZS24.

would be counter productive. As a result Churchill instructed with immediate effect both that all British forces left in France should be withdrawn, and that the B.E.F. be cancelled. One ship carrying 88th H.A.A Regiment equipment had, however, already reached Brest by the time the cancellation was issued. It was instructed as a matter of some urgency, before it had had the opportunity to unload, to return, but whilst in Brest to take on board two companies of Sherwood Foresters as part of the evacuation. Meanwhile the ships carrying troops from Plymouth had not yet departed, being moored on the harbour boom and ready to sail. They were instructed to return to their berths and disembark, the Regiment returning once again to their positions in the I.A.Z. on 18 June. On 22 June France signed an armistice with Germany.

Having re-established themselves in the I.A.Z., the Regiment received a warning order on 25 June that they would be moving to the Brockworth area of Gloucester, the Regiment relocating there on 27 June. Here the Regiment came under the control of 5 A.A. Division, John's battery being based at Haydons Elm[72] north of Gloucester. It was in Gloucestershire that John was allocated to A.A. training, transferring to 205 A.A. Training Regt on 15 August 1940, moving to Arborfield Garrisons. Here, and at Weybourne gunnery range, he trained 349 Battery to operational standards, it returning on completion, with John promoted to Sergeant, to 76th H.A.A. Regt from which it had originated as a cadre unit.

The 76th H.A.A. Regiment had originally been raised in 1859 as the Gloucestershire Volunteer Artillery, subsequently being reformed as 66th (South Midland) Field Brigade T.A. after World War I. In the restructuring of 1936 the regiment was designated as 76th A.A. Brigade, later becoming 76th H.A.A. Regiment R.A. under the umbrella of 46th A.A. Brigade, this in turn being part of 5th A.A. Division headquartered in Reading. In February 1941 46th A.A. Brigade was reallocated to 8th A.A. Division.

The 76th H.A.A. Regt was initially deployed in 1939 to defend Bristol, encompassing the city, docks, and the Bristol Aeroplane Company factory at Filton. After returning to 76th H.A.A Regt from training 349

---

[72] Gun site reference A12.

Ever your own, Johnnie, Britain, 1938-42

Battery was immediately deployed in Bristol on 11 November 1940. Initially with no guns, the battery was at first quartered at 'Bristol 12' at Hanham, but was very soon relocated to gun site 'Bristol 10' at Almondsbury, where it received four 3" semi mobile guns. Almost at once it was in action against the first large scale air raid on Bristol on the night of Sunday 24 November by 135 Luftwaffe aircraft. The raiders flew from bases in France using both *Knickebein* and the more sophisticated *Y Verfahen* radio signal navigation, dropping over 150 tons of high explosive bombs and 12,500 incendiaries targeted on the city docks. Two hundred people were killed and 689 injured as a result of the raid. The fires caused by the bombing inflicted significant damage to the centre of Bristol and could be seen from over 100 miles away[73]. Two Luftwaffe aircraft failed to return to their bases after the raid, but neither was directly attributed to the 3,400 heavy anti-aircraft rounds fired that night by Bristol's batteries. One plane came down in Cornwall, the other near the Isle of Wight as a result of A.A. fire from Portsmouth on its return flight. Despite cloud cover, the Luftwaffe returned on the night of 2 December, again using radio navigation, 121 aircraft dropping over 120 tons of bombs and 22,000 incendiaries. Whilst one aircraft crashed on take off killing all on board, all other aircraft returned to their bases despite heavy anti-aircraft fire. A further raid of sixty-seven planes took place on December 6th, with the aircraft approaching from the east, and dropping some 75 tons of bombs and over 5,500 incendiaries.

Following these attacks the defence of Bristol was reassessed and reorganised to improve its effectiveness on the approaches to the City. This resulted in 349 Battery, one of only two batteries with semi mobile guns (the remaining six sites using static guns), moving two of its 3" guns on 3 December from 'Bristol 10' Almondsbury to 'Bristol 12' at Hanham. These subsequently returned once again to Almondsbury on 18 December after new 3.7" mobile guns arrived to equip the batteries another regiment defending Bristol. Following further relocation of the 3" guns between Almondsbury and Hanham

---

[73] Rubble from this and subsequent raids was used as ballast on empty supply ships returning to the U.S., it being off loaded in New York near East 25th Street in an area to be known as the Bristol Basin, and commemorated with a plaque in 1942.

on 4 January 1941, 349 Battery was re-equipped with eight new 3.7" mobile guns on 30 January, four of these being located at 'Bristol 7' Whitchurch, and the remainder at 'Bristol 12' Hanham, where they stayed until late April.

The Luftwaffe raided Bristol again on 3 January 1941 with 178 aircraft, followed by a further raid, principally targeting Avonmouth, on 16 January of 126 aircraft, one of which was shot down by Cardiff based anti-aircraft fire. Another aircraft failed to return, and was assumed to have crashed into the sea. Luftwaffe activity during February was considerably less, being principally single aircraft raids. One of these was brought down by 236 Battery 76th H.A.A. Regiment on 22 February firing from Gordano, this being the second and last aircraft verified as directly attributable to heavy anti-aircraft fire from Bristol batteries during the war. Individual diaries by battery members, however, make more significant claims, these probably relating to successes by the R.A.F. Whilst the formal record may seem a small return for the considerable number of rounds fired, the effect of intense heavy anti-aircraft fire at enemy aircraft resulted in aircraft flying higher, taking evasive action, or turning away to avoid barrages, making their bombing less accurate, reducing the potential for and actual destruction of key target areas. The effect of the gunfire also, importantly, broke up Luftwaffe formations, making individual aircraft more vulnerable to attack by the R.A.F., as well as shell bursts drawing the attention of fighters to the presence of enemy aircraft that they may otherwise not have identified.

Heavy enemy raids resumed on 16 March when 167 aircraft bombed Bristol, followed by a further large raid on 3 April by 76 aircraft, during which bombs fell on 236 Battery's site at Gordano killing one and injuring five, and also damaging equipment. On the following night of 4 April 85 aircraft raided, a bomb falling on 238 Battery at Brickfields, killing one, whilst a second was killed by machine gun fire. The last significant raid on Bristol occurred on the night of 11 April with 153 aircraft dropping 190 tons of bombs and nearly 37,000 incendiaries targeting the docks and industrial areas, resulting in 180 deaths.

Sites in the Bristol area received further additional guns during April as well as new gun sites being opened and manned by batteries from 112 and 116 H.A.A. Regiments, a total of 66 heavy anti-aircraft guns now being deployed. Further reorganisation took place during May providing a total of twenty sites, these all being given new reference numbers. 349 Battery was located at this time at the newly numbered Whitchurch 'Bristol 17' site and 'Bristol 18' at Chew, both to the south of Bristol. They remained in these positions defending against ongoing but infrequent small scale raids by the Luftwaffe until 6 September when the Battery relocated to 'Bristol 3' Gordano, and 'Bristol 4' St George's Wharf. Improved G.L.II radar was delivered in August. In June John was promoted to Battery Sergeant Major (B.S.M./W.O.II) of 349 Battery, having been transferred from gun crew to Battery Headquarters (B.H.Q.) staff on 7 April.

On 6 October 1941 76th H.A.A. Regiment relocated to Weymouth, with the exception of 237 Battery, which moved to Dover, it subsequently rejoining the Regiment in Weymouth in January 1942. 349 Battery occupied gun sites adjacent to Nothe Fort, Wyke to the west, and Southwell on Portland Bill, R.H.Q. being based at Nottington House. Luftwaffe activity and associated anti-aircraft action on these sites was significantly less than that experienced in Bristol, despite the presence of the Whiteways Royal Navy Torpedo Factory and the harbour, raids mostly being single aircraft intrusions. On 22 October 238 Battery passed to War Office Control in preparation for overseas service, ceasing to be part of the Regiment.

Over the first three months of 1942 the Regiment underwent an intense period of mobility training for overseas service as part of the Military Reserve Roster, this, during March, being at Blandford Military Camp under 11 Brigade and the A.A. Mobility and Tactical Training Centre, and thereafter during April and May at Havant. On completion, the Regiment moved once more, this time to Gravesend as part of the outer defence to the Port of London, occupying sites at Strood, Green St. Green, and Jeskins Court, the location affording the opportunity for two batteries to undergo anti-tank gunnery practice at the anti-tank range at Foulness.

The Regiment moved to Dover on 3 July 1942, 349 Battery occupying positions at Farthingloe, D1, and Hope Farm, Hawkinge, D11, B.H.Q. being located at the former, a four gun emplacement on the White Cliffs to the west of the town, to defend against continuing raids and reconnaissance flights. In addition to air raids, Dover (and Folkestone to a lesser extent) was subjected to shelling by nineteen large enemy guns of up to 16" calibre located at seven static locations in France, as well as by mobile railway mounted guns. The guns were deployed principally to attack Allied shipping in the Channel, but also, by shelling the mainland, to demoralise the onshore British population. The first shells landed on 12 August 1940, a total of 2,226 being fired up to 26 September 1944 when the last guns were silenced following the D-Day invasion. In the face of the shelling the population of Dover shrank to half its pre-war size through evacuation, whilst those that remained spent considerable periods of time in deep shelters. A government report found that shelling was more feared than bombing due to the lack of warning.

A warning instruction was received by the Regiment on 16 July from 71 Brigade that it would come under War Office Control on 10 August, the required mobilisation resulting from this order being completed as planned by 1 September. Batteries were relieved of their sites, John's B.H.Q. relocating to Acrise Place to the north of Dover on 26 September. From this time the Regiment's activities focused on preparation for overseas service, receiving new 3.7" Mk III guns, new Mk II G.L. radar sets, vehicles together with details for their 'desertification', equipment and stores, as well as integrating signals, workshop, and other personnel into the regiment. Intensive mobility and gunnery training followed up by exercises continued, culminating on 27 September with 236 Battery, including the regiment's C.O. Colonel T. Smith, beginning its move to Glasgow for embarkation for the invasion of North Africa, it landing in Algiers on 8 November as part of the assault party of 'Operation Torch'.

In November the incumbent R.S.M. of 76 H.A.A. Regt was found to be medically unfit for overseas service and was discharged, the vacancy being offered to John Kemp. The rank was subsequently formalised on 19 November 1942, allowing John only three days to take up the responsibility prior to the forthcoming mobilisation. On 23 November the Regiment arrived in Glasgow, boarding transport ships *Batory* and *Durban Castle* bound for North Africa. The convoy sailed from the Clyde on 27 November, the Regiment providing men on each watch during the voyage for their ship's anti-aircraft guns.

The Years After Britain, 1942-45

John arrived in Algiers on 6 December 1942, establishing R.H.Q. at El Biar, southwest of the town, the regiment providing anti-aircraft defences for airfields and Allied Forces Headquarters as part of 1st Army. From here it made its way east, being based successively at Bougie, Djedjelli, Le Kef, and Djebel Abiod before taking part in the final assault on Bizerte in support of the U.S. infantry II Corps. The regiment was amongst the first to enter the town on 8 May, subsequently setting up anti-aircraft defences north of the harbour. In the aftermath of the Axis surrender in North Africa, 76th H.A.A. Regt underwent further training and 'toughening up' in Tunisia for the forthcoming 'Operation Husky', the invasion of Sicily.

John landed in Syracuse, Sicily, on 20 July, his regiment providing anti-aircraft defences around the port and at nearby airfields before moving to Augusta and then northwards to Messina. It was at the end of this campaign that John contracted jaundice and was hospitalised, initially in Syracuse, but then subsequently being sent back to Algiers to free frontline hospital space in Sicily for potential casualties arising from the imminent mainland invasion of Italy.

John eventually rejoined his regiment at Bari, Italy, two months later, a period of time unnecessarily prolonged as a result of the complexities and inefficiencies of transferring him back to active service. On his return he found that he no longer held the rank of the R.S.M. of the regiment as he had not held this position on active service for the requisite period of time, one year, for this to be substantive. John had, therefore, to revert to his previously substantiated rank of B.S.M., being posted to 236 Battery.

The regiment was present in Bari at the time of the infamous Luftwaffe raid on the night of 2 December 1943 during which a U.S. ship, the *John Harvey*, containing munitions including mustard gas bombs, was hit, the resultant fire and explosion dispersing chemicals over a wide area, causing over 1,000 casualties around the port.

From Bari the regiment moved north to Cerignola to defend Allied airfields, before advancing to Rome and then to Piombino on the west coast. It was here in July 1944 that the Regiment learned that it was to be allocated to a field artillery role, it quickly taking up positions on the Pisa plain within 4,500yds of the front line to the south of the River Arno in support of the U.S. IV Corps, providing harassing fire and counter battery missions against the German army as it retreated north. The final assault commenced at the beginning of April 1945, the Regiment advancing northwards on the west coast before rapidly moving east to San Benedetto Po, the location where the Regiment found itself when Germany surrendered.

Following the cessation of hostilities 76th H.A.A. Regt moved to Piacenza, and from there to Pesaro where it was designated to guard duties at Cesenatico Prisoner of War camp. The Regiment was wound down from May 1945 onwards, eventually moving back to Bari in November before being transferred to 51st H.A.A. Regiment as part of the demobilisation process, 76th H.A.A. Regiment, Royal Artillery, being placed in 'suspended animation'.

John returned home on New Year's Eve 1945 to take up civilian life with his wife, and the daughter who was borne following his departure for North Africa some three years before. He was placed on the Royal Army Reserve, undertaking training in June 1951, before finally being fully discharged in June 1959. A testimonial on his release papers, dated 24 November 1945, and signed by Lt Colonel Watson, stated: "Exemplary conduct. Keen and conscientious Sergeant Major. Thoroughly reliable and always an asset to the Regiment."

Ever your own, Johnnie, Britain, 1938-42

Ever your own, Johnnie, Britain, 1938-42

Appendices

Appendix 1. H.A.A gun positions and locations occupied by 282/88 Bty and 349/76 Bty

Dates	Gun site reference and location	Map reference	Notes
282 Battery 88th H.A.A. R.A. Regt			
1 Sept – 21 Oct 39	ZW8 Hurlingham	TQ 252 758	
21 Oct – 1 Nov 39	Enfield/Waltham Abbey	Not known	Lewis gun positions.
1 Nov – 20 Nov 39	ZE18 Chingford (Queen Elizabeth)	TQ 393 951	
20 Nov 39 – 17 Apr 40	ZW3 Burnt Farm	TL 321 021	Extant site.
9 Apr – 17 Apr 40	Crickelwood	Not known	Lewis gun positions.
21 Apr – 15 May 40	ZE18 Chingford (formerly Queen Elizabeth) ZE13 Finsbury Park	TQ 393 951 TQ 317 875	
28 May – 8 Jun 40 18 Jun- 27 Jun 40	ZS24 Annerly Park	TQ 343 696	
27 Jun – (15 Aug 40)	A12 Haydons Elm B1 Barnwood A15 Parton	SO 901 239 SO 852 176 SO 863 204	John transferred to 207 Training Regt on 15 Aug.
349 Battery 76th H.A.A. R.A. Regt			
11 Nov – 25 Nov 40	B12/15* Hanham	ST 636 715	349 Battery posted to 76th H.A.A. Regt on 11 Nov.

Ever your own, Johnnie, Britain, 1938-42

Dates	Gun site reference and location	Map reference	Notes
25 Nov – 3 Dec 40	B10/9* Almondsbury Henbury Golf Club	ST 606 833 ST 565 781	Assumed location, site identification number not known.
3 Dec – 18 Dec 40	B10/9* Almondsbury B12/15* Hanham	ST 606 831 ST 636 715	
30 Jan – 6 Sep 40 18 May – 6 Sep 40	B7 Whitchurch 18 Chew	ST 604 683 ST 551 627	One building remains.
6 Sep – 8 Oct 41	B1/3* Gordano 4 St Georges Wharf	ST 525 747 ST 501 711	Extant site.
8 Oct 41 – 23 Mar 42	Weymouth 1 2 Nothe Fort Weymouth 2 5 Wyke Weymouth 5 4 Southwell	SY 685 787 SY 658 776 SY 684 697	
23 Mar – 31 Mar 42	Blandford Forum Training Camp		
1 Apr – 15 May 42	Bedhampton Camp No 2, Havant		
15 May – 19 Jun 42	Jeskins Court Green Street Green Strood	Not known TQ 590 708 Not known	Site reference numbers not known.
19 Jun – 3 July 42	TS15 Cobham	TQ 676 682	
7 Jul -26 Sept 42	D1 Farthingloe D11 Hawkinge	TR 297 399 TR 207 420	Extant site.

* pre-reorganisation of site locations site number/post reorganisation site number.

Gordano gun battery, B1/3, Happerton Farm, Bristol (2013)

One of the gun pits, looking towards Bristol Channel.

Access to, and detail of, one of two ammunition magazines.

Farthingloe gun battery, D1, White Cliffs, Dover (2013)

A gun pit, showing ammunition lockers and generator accommodation. The tree is located on the gun position.

Site building, possibly B.H.Q.

Fuze inventory board.

The English Channel and distant view of France seen from the battery.

Appendix 2. The Vickers QF 3.7 inch Anti-Aircraft Gun

Two configurations of the Vickers 3.7" QF gun were produced, being mobile and static. Mobile guns were fitted with a limber and carriage, each on two pairs of inflatable tyres, and four folding outriggers with levelling jacks to provide a mounting for the gun when in use. The carriage wheels to the front of the gun were raised when the gun was readied for action, being used as a counterweight. These could alternatively be removed, as with the rear limber set, this becoming standard practice later in the war. The gun mounting required to be precisely levelled before accurate firing could be achieved. The static gun was generally mounted on a concrete base in a permanent gun emplacement.

At the outset of World War II gun batteries each comprised four guns, but soon increased to eight guns, three batteries making up a heavy anti-aircraft (H.A.A.) regiment, providing a total of twenty four guns. A battery's guns were divided into two equal sized Troops, each being designated a letter from A to F for the six troops comprising the regiment.

For a gun to be fired one of two members of the gun crew designated as loaders would bring a shell to the gun and, after the shell's fuze had been set, place the shell in the loading tray. The tray was then swung into line with the open breech and the round rammed home with the wire rope ramming device. The action of ramming home the round closed the breech and operated the firing-pin in the breech block. The breech would not close fully until the loading tray was returned to its original position. A breech lever was used when the gun was fired first, the gun operating automatically thereafter.

When the gun fired the recoil was absorbed by a cylinder of compressed air. This brought the gun to rest, returning it to its firing position whilst simultaneously opening the breech and ejecting the empty cartridge case. It was found when using the gun at a low elevation in a ground shooting role, as opposed to the higher angles required in typical anti-aircraft usage, that more air would be drawn into the recoil buffer resulting in a shorter and more violent recoil which could make the gun 'jump' out of position. The violence of the recoil was reduced by slackening off the air cylinder's release plugs.

Permanent anti-aircraft gun emplacements were constructed as octagonal enclosures, usually of concrete or brick, one face commonly being left open for access, and with a central mounting for a static gun. Four emplacements, sufficient for one battery, were constructed in an arc around a central control. Each emplacement contained ammunition lockers built against the enclosure walls, together with a generator bunker to power the gun equipment. Temporary emplacements often used sandbags to enclose the gun position.

In a ground shooting role the guns were usually positioned in temporary pits, wooden pickets up to 4 feet in length being driven into the ground around the mounting to prevent the gun from slewing or shifting, this being a common problem due to the recoil when using a gun at low elevation. This did not, however, prevent the gun 'jumping' when fired and the resultant potential for the gun to move out of position, the gun requiring regular re-levelling and calibration. It was also recommended that gun mountings be regularly rotated to minimise wear due to the gun recoil.

Guns were moved between locations using gun tractor vehicles, commonly AEC Matador or Scammell, capable of towing the gun at up to 30 mph on a good road. They were also able to tow across open country.

The Vickers QF 3.7 inch Anti-Aircraft Gun Specification.

Production period	1937–1945
Number produced	approx 10,000
Weight	9 tons 12 cwt (9.75 tonnes)
Length	16 ft 3 in (4.95m)
Width	8 ft 0 in (2.45m)
Barrel length	15 ft 5 in (4.69m)
Gun crew	7 – 10[74]
Weight of shell[75]	49 lb (22 kg)
Calibre	3.7" (94 mm)
Elevation	-5° to +80°
Traverse	360°
Rate of fire	hand loading: 8 rounds per minute
	auto-loading: 19 rounds per minute
Mobile mountings	Mk I, and Mk III variants.
Static mountings (fixed)	Mk II, and Mk VI variants.
Muzzle velocity, Mk I-III[76]	(new barrel) 2,670 ft/s (814 m/s)
	(worn barrel) 2,598 ft/s (792 m/s)
Muzzle velocity, Mk VI[77]	3,425 ft/s (1,044 m/s)
Maximum horizontal range	20,000 yds (11 miles/18.2 km)
Ceiling	Mk I, II 32,000 ft (9,750 m)
	Mk VI 50,000 ft (15,240 m)

---

[74] See page 150 for information on and composition of gun crews.
[75] Combined weight of shell, cartridge, and fuze.
[76] The Mk I gun utilised a monobloc barrel, whilst in the MkII and III the barrel was manufactured with a loose liner. The Mk IV and Mk V proved not to be viable designs, using a 4.5" barrel fitted with a liner to reduce the bore to 3.7"
[77] The Mk VI was a static gun, entering service in 1944

Ammunition

The ammunition used by the 3.7" Vickers gun was a fixed brass necked cartridge round, with shell and cartridge as one. Ammunition for anti-aircraft use was principally high explosive (H.E.), but shrapnel shells were also used against low flying aircraft, each utilising a time fuze. In a field role percussion fuzes could be used in addition to time fuzes.

Examples of fuzes used:

Fuze No.199: powder-burning, with a maximum running time of 30 seconds: range limited to 9,000 yds in ground shooting.
Fuze No. 207: mechanical, range limited to 16,000 yds in ground shooting, but often in short supply.
Fuze No. 208: mechanical, maximum running time of 43 seconds.
Fuze No. 223: time and percussion fuze.
Fuze No. 232: percussion fuze.

The 199 Fuze burning rate was found to be variable, in particular with altitude, giving inconsistent timings and making it unreliable, leading to the introduction of mechanical fuzes. 199 Fuzes were usually sorted into batches and calibrated to provide greater consistency.

The initiation of a fuze's timing was triggered by the acceleration of the shell as a result of the gun being fired. Care was needed in loading shells; carrying or holding a shell by the fuze could result in the loader inadvertently moving the fuze from its 'safe' position, a particular risk with 208 Fuzes, with the potential for a subsequent 'premature' detonation and gun crew casualties.

A major advance in 1942 was the introduction of Machine Fuze Setter No.11, on Mounting Mk. IIC, a gun that also introduced fully powered laying, loading and fuze setting, and Carriage Mk. IIIA, raising the potential rate of fire to 20 rounds per minute. In ground shooting, however, this rate of fire had to be considerably reduced to prevent the barrel from overheating and distorting.

A used 199 fuze, less its timing ring, found as debris by Peggy Kemp after a night of anti-aircraft activity when returning home from night duty at the local A.R.P. ambulance station. It was subsequently used as a doorstop.

The Gun Crew

The Vickers A.A. guns were each manned by a gun crew of up to ten men, or of women or mixed crews later in the War, under the command of a commissioned Gun Position Officer (G.P.O) and a Gun Position Officer Assistant (G.P.O.A.). At the outset of the war the troops operating the gun in an A.A. role were frequently divided as follows:

No.1 Commander (N.C.O.)
No.2 Gun layer for line.
No.3 Gun layer for elevation.
No.4 Fuze setter.
No.5 Breech operator.
No.6 Rammer.
No.7 Loader.
No.8 Loader.
No.9 Fuze setter operator.
No.10 Ammunition supplier.

When the gun, Mk. III, was used in a field role from 1944 onwards, the gun crew was commonly:

No.1 Commander (N.C.O.)
No.2 Gun layer for line.
No.3 Gun layer for elevation.
No.4 Fuze setter.
No.5 loading and firing.
No.6 loading and firing.
No.7 not used.
No.8 not used.
No.9 Calling corrected fuze (omitted if 208 fuze being used).

Predictor

The predictor calculated the bearing and elevation of the gun, and the fuze setting of the shell so that it would detonate in proximity of the target. The calculation took account of the wind curve of the trajectory and barometric pressure, the resultant data being transmitted to the guns through electrical cables. The need for this equipment was plainly very important when taking into consideration that an aircraft of the time flying at 30,000 ft would have flown two miles in the thirty seconds it would take an A.A. round to attain a similar height.

Predictors first came into service in the 1920s, with the Vickers No.1. Development and refinement continued from this date to the end of WWII, with eleven variants seeing service from differing manufacturers, including Vickers, Sperry, Kerrison, and Bell.

3. 76th H.A.A. Regt R.A. structure within the Army

At the outset of WWII, the 76th H.A.A. Regiment R.A. comprised three batteries, being 236, 237, and 238, 238 later leaving the Regiment, being replaced by 349 Battery. The batteries were each subdivided into two troops, being designated A, B; C, D; and E, F respectively. Each of the batteries were under the command of their respective Battery Headquarters (B.H.Q.). A Major was responsible for each Battery as Officer Commanding (O.C.) supported by Captains, and Lieutenants/Subalterns, and who in turn were supported by a Battery Sergeant Major (B.S.M./W.O.II), and N.C.O.s.

The Regiment was commanded through Regimental Headquarters (R.H.Q.), comprising the Commanding Officer (C.O), usually a Colonel, together with a team of commissioned officers, a Regimental Sergeant Major (R.S.M./W.O.I), and N.C.O.s.

Regiments were usually homogeneous units fixed by type and normally not self-sufficient when operating in the field. H.A.A. Regiments could be allocated to duties alongside other diverse Regiments, these collectively creating a Brigade, under the direction of a Colonel, Brigadier, or Brigadier General. A Brigade was most often a unit of various regiments (e.g. infantry, tanks, and artillery) created for a specific campaign purpose. The organisation of a Brigade was flexible, and could operate independently in the field.

Several Brigades could be assembled to form a Division, under the direction of a Major General. Divisions could be assembled into Corps commanded by a Lieutenant General, Corps in turn making up Armies, for example 8th Army, as commanded by Field Marshal Montgomery.

Principal references

History of the Royal Regiment of Artillery, Anti-Aircraft Artillery 1914 – 55: Brigadier N.W. Routledge, OBE. TD

War Office War Diaries and other documents

W.O. 32/4685 – Specification of 3.7" AA gun

W.O. 32/3359 – Specification of a new AA gun QF

W.O. 166/2245– Headquarters 26 Anti-aircraft Brigade, General (HQ G) 1 Aug 1939 – 31 Dec 1940

W.O. 166/2287 – 46 AA Brigade, Sept 1939-Dec 1940

W.O. 166/2367 – 76th HAA Regiment, August 1939 to December 1941

W.O. 166/2379 – 88th HAA Regiment War Diary, August 1939 to May 1941

W.O. 166/2561 – 282 Battery 88 HAA 23 August 1939 - March 1941

W.O. 166/7453 – 76th Heavy A.A. Regiment, R.A., 1 Jan - 31 October 1942

W.O. 167/617 – 53 Heavy Anti-aircraft (HAA) Regt Royal Artillery 1 Aug 1939-30 June 1940

W.O. 204/8336 – A Brief History of 76th H.A.A. Regt R.A.

Internet

Bristol Historical Resource   humanities.uwe.ac.uk/bhr/main

Aircrew Remembered   aircrewremembered.com

Glossary of common WWII military abbreviations

A.A.	anti-aircraft
A.A.D.C.	Anti-Aircraft Defence Commander
A.A.O.R.	Anti-Aircraft Operations Room
a/c	aircraft
A.C.C.	Army Catering Corps
Ack Ack	anti-aircraft
Adj	Adjutant
A.F.H.Q.	Allied Forces Headquarters
A.F.O.D.	Air Force Operations Detachment (US)
A.F.S.C.	Air Force Systems Command (US)
A/G	airgraph
A.G.R.A	Army Group Royal Artillery
a/m	aforementioned
A/M	airmail
A.P.O.	Army Post Office
A.P.S.	Army Postal Service
A.R.P.	Air Raids Precautions
A.S.A.C.	Air Service Area Command (US)
A.T.S.	Auxiliary Territorial Service
Bde	Brigade
Bdr	Bombardier
B.C.	Battery Commander
B.E.F.	British Expeditionary Force
B.F.N.A.	British Forces in North Africa
B.H.Q.	Battery headquarters
B.L.A.	British Liberation Army

B.N.A.F	British North Africa Forces
B.S.M	Battery Sergeant Major (W.O. II)
Brig	Brigadier
Btn	Battalion
Bty	Battery
B.Q.M.S.	Battery Quarter Master Sergeant
Captn	Captain
C.C.S.	Casualty Clearing Station
C.D.	Civil Defence
C.O.	Commanding Officer
Coy	Company
C.M.F.	Central Mediterranean Forces
Cmdr	Commander
C.M.P.	Corp of Military Police
C.P.	Command Post
Cpl	Corporal
C.S.M.	Company Sergeant Major (W.O.II)
C.W.	chemical weapon(s)
D.A.D.O.S	Deputy Assistant Director of Ordnance Services
D.O.	Dental Officer
D.R.	Despatch Rider
E.N.S.A.	Entertainments International Services Association
F.B.	flying bomb
F.W.	Focke-Wulf
G.C.I.	Ground Controlled Interception
G.D.A.	Gun Defended Area
G.H.Q.	General Headquarters
G.I.	Government Issue, but when applied to soldiers short for "G I Joe", an American soldier
G.L.	gun laying radar
G.O.R.	Gun Operations Room
Gnr	Gunner
G.P.	gun park
G.T.V	gun tractor vehicle

H.A.A.	heavy anti-aircraft
H.E.	high explosive
He	Heinkel
H.G.	Home Guard
H.Q.	Headquarters
I.A.Z.	Inner Artillery Zone
i/c	in charge/command
2 i/c	second in command
int	intelligence
K.D.	khaki drill/drab
L.A.A.	Light Anti-aircraft
L/B or L/Bdr	Lance Bombardier
L.M.G.	light machine gun
L.I.A.P.	leave in addition to Python
L.I.L.O.P	leave in lieu of Python
L.S.T.	Landing Ship Tank
L.C.I.	Landing Craft Infantry
Lt	Lieutenant
Lt/Col	Lieutenant Colonel
L/Cpl	Lance Corporal
Mat	AEC Matador gun tractor
M/C	motorcycle
M.C.	Master of Ceremonies
Me	Messerschmitt
M/G	machine gun
M.O.	Medical Officer
M.P.	Military Police
M.T.	motor transport
M.V.	motor vehicle
P.O.W.	Prisoner of War
P.R.	Post Room
N.A.	North Africa

N.A.A.F	Northwest African Airforce
N.A.A.F.I.	Navy Army Airforce Institute
N.A.A.S.C.	North African Air Service Command (US)
N.C.O.	Non Commissioned Officer
N.O.I.C.	Naval Officer in Command
O.C.	Officer Commanding
O.P.	observation post
O.C.T.U.	Officer Cadet Training Unit
O.R.	other ranks
O.T.C	Officer Training Corp
P.A.D.	Passive Air Defense
P.O.	Post Office
Pte	Private
Q or Q.M.	Quartermaster
R.A.	Royal Artillery
R.A.S.C.	Royal Army Service Corps
R.B.	Rifle Brigade
R.C.S.	Royal Corps of Signals
R.D.F.	Range and Direction Finding
R.E.	Royal Engineers
Regt	Regiment
R.E.M.E.	Royal Electrical and Mechanical Engineers
R.H.Q.	Regimental Headquarters
R.P.	Regimental Paymaster
R.S.M.	Regimental Sergeant Major (W.O. I)
R.T.O.	Railway Transportion Office
Sectn	Section
Sgt	Sergeant
Sgm	Sergeant Major
S.L.	searchlight
S.O.R.	Sector Operations Room
Sub/Lt	Sub Lieutenant
T.A.	Territorial Army

Tiffys	Artificers (motor mechanics)
Tp or Trp	Troop
U.D.F.I.	Union Defence Forces Institute
U.S.A.F.	United States Airforce
V.A.	vulnerable area
V.P.	vulnerable point
W.A.C.	Women's Army Corp (US)
W.D.	War Department
W/L	wagon lines
W.O.	Warrant Officer
W.O.L.	without leave
W.R.N.S.	Women's Royal Navy Service
W/T	wireless transmitter
YMCA	Young Men's Christian Association

L - #0137 - 070120 - C0 - 210/148/9 - PB - DID2733424